FRESH FRUIT

FRESH FRUIT

MEDITATIONS ON THE FRUIT OF THE HOLY SPIRIT

Jennifer Chamberlain

Fresh Fruit

Published by Inscript Publishing
P.O. Box 611
Bladensburg, MD 20710-0611
www.inscriptpublishing.com

Cover Design by Raenita Wiggins
Cover Art by Miriam Clark

Library of Congress Control Number: 2018940383

ISBN: 978-0-9986690-9-0

Printed in the United States of America

Table of Contents

Introduction

Fresh Fruit is a collection of writings that show ways the fruit of the Holy Spirit can teach us and give help and encouragement as we face everyday problems of life.

There are nine categories, one for each fruit. Each fruit has eight compositions, each followed by a prayer, regarding issues we face in life and how the fruit of the Holy Spirit can help us.

As Christians, we have a helper given to us by Christ. The Holy Spirit was given to us to guide, direct, educate, encourage and help us with our struggles. The Holy Spirit's presence is what sets us apart in this world.

Without recognizing how important the fruit of the Holy Spirit are in our lives, we are not fully experiencing all God offers us. We become spiritually healthier by asking God for His fruit.

Good plants produce good fruit. Our Lord used the analogy of the fruit to describe the emotions, temperaments, and skills with which He builds us up through His Holy Spirit. He wants us to grow into good plants.

Life is challenging for everyone; the rich, the poor, the religious, and the non-religious. We are all equal when it comes to having struggles even though we may not notice them in each other.

God the Father, God the Son, and God the Holy Spirit are one. When we ask for the fruit of the Holy Spirit, we receive them from Him.

We receive them for our own use and to use with others. We can show them to the world through the way we live and the way we react to our challenges. Through these fruit, we can show whom God is and hopefully produce good fruit in the lives of others that will bring them to salvation.

I have written Fresh Fruit so that each topic can be read separately, or the entire book can be read at once.

All scripture, unless otherwise noted, is from the English Standard Version Bible. Definitions are from Strong's Concordance.

May God Richly Bless You!

Jenni

About the Holy Spirit

But the Helper, the Holy Spirit, whom the Father will send in my name, he will teach you all things and bring to your remembrance all that I have said to you (John 14:26).

Jesus said that the Holy Spirit would be a helper to us after He was crucified, raised and ascended again to the Father. He told the disciples that the Holy Spirit would bring to their remembrance everything that He had taught them.

The disciples were with Jesus day and night and heard His word, but we, his modern-day disciples, must read or hear the word before it can be brought back to our remembrance. Time spent reading God's word is how we learn and grow in the knowledge of the Father. The Holy Spirit makes God's word come alive to us and helps us to remember what we learn.

Nevertheless, I tell you the truth: it is to your advantage that I go away, for if I do not go away, the Helper will not come to you. But if I go, I will send him to you. And when he comes, he will convict the world concerning sin and righteousness and judgment: concerning sin, because they do not believe in me; concerning righteousness, because I go to the Father, and you will see me no longer; concerning judgment, because the ruler of this world is judged (John 16:7-11).

Jesus said that the Holy Spirit will convict the world of sin. It is our conscience, telling us right from wrong. We need to listen to what God is telling us through His Holy Spirit because we are judged in the end.

When we accept Christ as our savior, knowing that He saved us by dying in our place, we receive the Holy Spirit. Everything God offers is free to us because Christ paid the price in advance.

The Holy Spirit gives us His fruit when we ask for them, and they become part of us so that we can produce good fruit in the world. If we seek the fruit of the spirit, we will also show these fruit in our behavior. We can share these fruit and help others to seek them through Jesus Christ, our savior.

> **And I will give you a new heart, and a new spirit I will put within you. And I will remove the heart of stone from your flesh and give you a heart of flesh (Ezekiel 36:26).**

Love:
The first fruit of the Holy Spirit

But the fruit of the Spirit is love, joy, peace, patience, kindness, goodness, faithfulness, gentleness, self-control; against such things there is no law. And those who belong to Christ Jesus have crucified the flesh with its passions and desires.

If we live by the Spirit, let us also keep in step with the Spirit (Galatians 5:22-25).

Agape is the ancient Greek word which refers to the highest form of love; the love of God for man and of man for God.

Love is the theme of the entire Bible. God is love, and everything else flows from that love.

Because of His great love for us, God will not allow sin to stand between Him and His creation. He personally bridged the separation by sending His son.

Hearing that Jesus had silenced the Sadducees, the Pharisees got together. One of them, an expert in the law, tested him with this question: "Teacher, which is the greatest commandment in the Law?"

Jesus replied: "'Love the Lord your God with all your heart and with all your soul and with all your mind.' This is the first and greatest commandment. And the second is like it: 'Love your neighbor as yourself.' All the Law and the Prophets hang on these two commandments" (Matthew 22:34-40 NIV).

The God of Love

Anyone who does not love does not know God, because God is love (1 John 4:8).

God's love is pure, and He is pure love. His word, the Bible, is one long love story all about His love for us. This love is not based on anything we can do. There is no way to earn it. It just is, and He loves us just as we are. Not only does He love those who believe in Him, but all of His children, everyone, everywhere, even those who have not come to know Him yet.

God calls us sons and daughters and heirs to His kingdom. We are His family. There is no greater joy than being a part of the family of God and experiencing His love. There is no way for us as human beings to understand something so deep and never-ending. His love is not like our love; it is completely unselfish and free. That is why, even after we brought sin into the world, He still loved us and sent His son to make it right.

As pure love, God listens to our cares, hurts, and struggles. He empathizes and comforts us and works all things for our good. Our Father knows us by name and cares about every detail of our lives. His love is beyond measure. Human love can be lost, but God's love is eternal.

And we know that for those who love God all things work together for good, for those who are called according to his purpose (Romans 8:28).

Love that comes to us from the Father also needs to flow through us back to Him and out of us to others. It is not a one-way street. Because we have such a Father, and such a blessed love, it is important to share. That is what this fruit is all about. Being loved like this, we cannot keep it to ourselves. Not only should we return God's love, but we should be showing it to the world. If we don't, they will never experience this type of love. This type of love is impossible in this lost and dying world.

A new commandment I give to you, that you love one an-

other: just as I have loved you, you also are to love one another (John 13:24).

The world does not have this love for each other and they don't understand that God loves them just as they are. We need to tell them. He can't help it. He is love and they are His children. It doesn't matter where they are, what they have done, or what they are doing. He loves them. He loves everyone.

See what kind of love the Father has given to us, that we should be called children of God; and so we are. The reason why the world does not know us is that it did (does) not know him (1 John 3:1, Jenni's paraphrase).

Though it makes no human sense why the Creator of the universe would care so much about us, He has told us it is so, and we know it in our innermost being. We understand that everyone is important to Him. Let us care about others with this love from God, not as the world loves, but as God loves. Love shown to others can never go wrong.

In our daily prayers, ask God for the ability to show His love to others through the work of the Holy Spirit. Ask for a great measure of this fruit to flow through you. This mystery of God's love may not be understood, but we feel it and rejoice.

Beloved, let us love one another, for love is from God, and whoever loves has been born of God and knows God. (1 John 4:7).

We love because he first loved us (1 John 4:19).

Prayer: **Lord, let us love one another as you love us. Though it is impossible for us to understand your great love, let us show it through our lives. Don't let us forget that you love everyone just as they are. No one is required to be perfect before coming to you. You are love. Amen.**

Loneliness

A new commandment I give to you, that you love one another: just as I have loved you, you also are to love one another (John 13:34).

The God of Love commanded us to love each other. We are not alone, and we know we are loved because God and our Christian brothers and sisters love us. But are we aware of those who are lonely, and don't feel loved? Do we show God's love to them?

We all feel alone sometimes. We may have secrets that cause us to separate ourselves, or are ashamed of our past, so we hide out and allow ourselves to be lonely. We may believe we are different from everyone else and no one understands or likes us. We may just be shy and uncomfortable in large groups, so we don't make friends easily. Loneliness is a painful and confusing place, and we all experience it.

We Christians are the worst at letting people know that we are feeling lonely. If no one reaches out to us, we begin to doubt our likeability, which makes us feel lonelier. Whether it is our turn to feel lonely or not, we need to reach out to others.

When we feel alone, it is especially important to reach out to other Christians, not wait for them to reach out to us. Whether we are just lonely or whether we are going through something difficult, it is important to share with others who believe as we do. There are blessings for both the sharer and the one who helps to bear the burden.

If our feelings of aloneness are brought on because of situations in our daily lives, such as living alone, not having any close friends, financial burdens, or family burdens, we can find rest in the Lord and know that He is working in our lives. We can feel His love through the love of others. Feeling that God has abandoned us and that our prayers are unheard is a lonely feeling indeed.

God is unchanging and never moves away from us. He is everywhere and everything always. When we feel lost, alone and far away from God, it is we who have moved. His word says, 'come to me.' With each movement we make toward God, the less lonely we will feel.

When we look at those around us, we may believe that they have everything together. They seem to be super Christians, never feel alone or depressed, have great families, and plenty of money. We envy them and sometimes can feel a little bitter because of their supposed success in life. Interestingly enough, they may think the same about us.

What we see and feel about other people is normally not true. Take the time to get to know them, and we find that they have struggles just like we do. It is no wonder we feel alone when we think everyone else is doing so well. Only when we look outside of ourselves will we really feel that we have companionship, and the great love of God.

> **Bear one another's burdens, and so fulfill the law of Christ (Galatians 6:2).**

Christians should be the best at loving each other and being helpful. We know that bearing each other's burdens makes our own burdens lighter. However, we often don't notice when others are feeling alone. We can't take our eyes off our own problems or stop worrying about what people might be thinking of us long enough to look around and see how others might be suffering.

Instead of worrying about what we are wearing or how we look or talk, we should be watching for those who are not participating in groups or not in attendance. Self-focus blinds us to the burdens others are carrying.

> **So whatever you wish that others would do to you, do also to them, for this is the Law and the Prophets (Matthew 7:12).**

When we are lonely, what do we wish for from our friends? We want them to notice, to care for us, and to share their own experiences and how God helped them overcome. We can share our own feelings of insecurity, worry, or stress so that they feel comfortable opening up about their own. Sharing our experiences is much more easily accepted than advice.

Changing our own self-focused attitudes is not easy. Being able to connect in person, eye to eye, and giving hugs is difficult for many of us, but we can be a friend and not a 'know it all.' Asking ourselves what we would want is a good way to remember how to help those who are lonely.

> **Do nothing from rivalry or conceit, but in humility count others more significant than yourselves. Let each of you look not only to his own interests, but also to the interests of others (Philippians 2:3,4).**

Thinking of others before thinking of ourselves is not a natural part of human nature. To be able to truly love takes divine intervention and is something we must ask for from God.

As Christians, we have become new creatures, and the spiritual nature we receive from the Holy Spirit is more than able to carry out this task. Our old nature will try to take over and make us think of ourselves first, but Christ's example is to reach out to others.

> **Come to me, all who labor and are heavy laden, and I will give you rest (Matthew 11:28).**

We can come to Him when we are lonely. He is working out His plan in the lives of the lonely and those who are not. There are moments when we are not strong enough in our faith to feel His love when things are bad, but we know He is near, and we will feel it soon. In the meantime, we can rely on each other.

> ***Prayer:*** **Dear Lord, when we are feeling lonely, please come closer so that we can feel your love. Send us those who love you or send us someone who needs your love. You felt these feelings of loneliness on the cross, you know our pain and heartache. We love you Lord and thank you for always being with us no matter what. Amen.**

Christ, Our First Love

But I have this against you, that you have abandoned the love you had at first (Revelations 2:4).

Remembering when we first found Jesus and asked Him to come into our lives, it was such a feeling of elation. We asked Him to forgive our sins, and we felt so much love from Him and for Him. We were so excited we wanted to tell everyone about His great love.

When our sins were first forgiven, we knew how much we owed the Lord. His death on the cross was real and powerful to us. We knew how unworthy we were and knowing that Jesus loved us and died for us was almost unfathomable.

We all have a passion for different things at different times in our lives. Our passions come and go depending on what interests us or what has affected us in some way. Our greatest excitement is usually when something is new. As the newness wears off, the excitement tends to wane. Our passion and excitement for Christ can do the same.

Therefore, I tell you, her many sins have been forgiven--as her great love has shown. But whoever has been forgiven little loves little (Luke 7:47).

In the book of Luke, a woman who washed Christ's feet with her tears and anointed His feet with costly perfume was full of passion for the Lord. Her passion was great because Christ had forgiven her many sins. She knew how unworthy she was of this great love.

Unfortunately, as time passes, we lose our passion and excitement about what Jesus has done for us. Hopefully, it is not because we feel we owe Christ less than we did before. In our hearts, we know how unworthy we still are, but we excuse our lack of enthusiasm by saying that we have matured in Christ. We don't want to shout it to the world because it may offend someone. Justifying our lack of passion becomes easy, and we are in danger of becoming cold.

In Revelation 2:1-4, Jesus told the church at Ephesus that even though they were doing good works, were patient and hated evil, they had lost their first love of Him and needed to get that passion back. Was He speaking to us too?

This world is a chaotic place. We have jobs and families, struggles and fears, places to go, and people to see. It is easy to get so bogged down with life that our passion for Christ takes a back seat. Are we letting our daily life get in the way of abundant life?

Have we lost our first love?

We often talk about Christ dying for our sins, but do we think about what that really means? He died a horrendous death, even though it should have been us with nails through our hands and feet. Daily we sin and fall short of His glory, driving those nails deeper and deeper. We owe such a great debt, and we can only pay it with our lives, our love, and our passion.

No matter how long we have been Christians, we will never deserve what Christ has done for us. If we worked at it every minute for eternity, keeping Christ at the center of our lives, we would never be worthy of His undeserved death on the cross. The world is nothing, gives us nothing, and doesn't help us in any way. Only the love of God is life to us.

> **And you shall love the Lord your God with all your heart and with all your soul and with all your mind and with all your strength (Mark 12:30).**

It is clear what our instructions are, although many people struggle with the last part of this verse. We know how to turn our hearts toward God and to love Him and feel His love in our hearts and souls, but how do we love Him with our strength?

The Greek biblical definition of strength includes words such as ability, energy, and powerful deeds We can love God by using our abilities, energy, and deeds to make Him known to those around us. We can love God with all our strength.

Everything we have and everything we are is because God sent His son Jesus Christ to die in our place to give us abundant life now, and eternal life with Him. Let's invite God to be involved in all our other passions in life, instead of letting our other passions crowd out God. Stop the world from gradually creeping in by communicating more with Him and strengthening that relationship. God is pure love.

Life cannot be allowed to steal away our love and gratefulness for what He has done for us. If we make Him our first love, the rest of what we love will have more meaning.

Anyone who does not love does not know God, because God is love (1 John 4:8).

***Prayer*: Lord, we pray for ways that we can show our love for you and your love for us to everyone around us. We know that you love us more than we will ever know, and we want to have the excitement we knew when we first invited you into our hearts. Your love and your sacrifice are more than we can understand and with your help, we can return to our first love. Amen.**

The Assurance

Though he had done so many signs before them, they still did not believe in him ... And whereas he did all these miracles before them, they did not trust in him[1] ... he had done so many signs before them, yet they didn't believe in him[2] (John 12:37).

Salvation through faith is assured by God and His son Jesus Christ. It is real, but the devil is blinding the eyes of the world. The world is sick and dying.

We have seen and read about His signs, and we are assured that Christ is truth and love. The evil in the world hides the truth and works in lives to draw them away from God. It is no secret to us why people won't accept Him.

The world is worse in many ways now than it was when Christ walked this earth and performed miracles. Miracles like the ones He performed are not as prevalent because our faith is weak. We are assured of salvation when we ask Christ into our lives and hearts, but when trying to show this assurance to others, we run into those whose eyes have been blinded.

There are those who think God is a myth. They believe that the Bible and records of His life and death are not true. Therefore, they say, we would be idiots to believe.

If they truly listened and studied, not just the Bible, but scholars and old manuscripts and the prophecies that were fulfilled, they would know that God is not a myth.

Trying to assure people of God's salvation comes easiest after we develop a close relationship with them and they can see how God works in our lives. We can point out our experiences and the miraculous ways they are resolved.

Then there are those who know there is a God and that they should probably be following Him, but don't feel the time is right. Following

---

1 The Original Aramaic New Testament in Plain English- with Psalms & Proverbs Copyright © 2007; 8th edition Copyright © 2013
All rights reserved. Used by Permission.

2 Word English Bible, public domain

Him now would ruin their 'fun.' They think there is plenty of time to follow Him more closely later, and they think they are probably safe because they merely believe. They are not considering that the devil also believes, but will not have eternal life with God.

None of us are sure that we have tomorrow. At some point, it will be too late for those who keep putting their so-called pleasures before God. We need to show them that He gives joy, takes away burdens, leads, guides, strengthens and loves. They will never be sorry to give up what they think is 'fun' now for what God has for all of us.

There are also those who think we are all going to the same place when we die because we are all basically good. We can worship anything we want; any higher power will do. They believe that all religions are the same and may or may not be real.

> **Thus says the Lord, the King of Israel and his Redeemer, the Lord of hosts: "I am the first and I am the last; besides me there is no god" (Isaiah 44:6).**

We who believe in the Lord Jesus Christ know the plan that God, in His great love for us, has put in place to renew humankind's relationship with Him. We have a great responsibility to show that God is real. He is the only true God. Jesus is the only one who died in our place and rose from the dead. We are all sinners and deserved death, but He took the punishment, and only through Him can we be reconciled to God.

Today is the day for us to show God's love to the unlovely, His peace to the struggling, and His hope to the hopeless. All can be assured salvation through Jesus Christ by confessing their sins and asking Jesus to be their Lord and Savior.

> **Yet you do not know what your life will be like tomorrow. You are just a vapor that appears for a little while and then vanishes away (James 4:14).**

Life here is very short compared to eternity, but in it, we can have love, joy, peace, and so much more. Assurance of eternal life with God comes from knowing Jesus Christ and is not a secret for us to hold, but a gift to be shared with those who do not know Him yet.

Daily, we wonder why those around us don't call out to our marvelous God. But have we told them about Him or shown them His love? He is everywhere and works every second (as we understand time), to bring people into His loving arms. How great is His love for us and for all who call on His name.

We may live in a world of darkness and sorrow, but we do not have to partake of its pain. We have, not only a friend and brother, but a King and Lord, who has power and might, who will make good out of any bad thing that happens to us. He is God Almighty and yet, He loves and is gentle, allowing everyone the free choice of whether to accept the assurance of His love, His care, and His eternal life. This is what we can share.

No matter how the world may view us, we have what others want. The world is searching for assurances. There is a void that only Christ can fill. We can rejoice that we have God's assurance and we need to share it.

> **Jesus said to him, "I am the way, and the truth, and the life. No one comes to the Father except through me" (John 14:6).**

> ***Prayer:*** **Lord, there are mysteries and scriptures that we may not understand, but help us tell our own stories of who we were before we found you, and how you saved us. Help us share your love and how you work in our lives daily. We are willing Lord. Help us to show the assurance of eternal life with you. Amen.**

The Benefits of Being a Christian

Give, and it will be given to you. Good measure, pressed down, shaken together, running over, will be put into your lap. For with the measure you use it will be measured back to you (Luke 6:38).

The biggest benefit of being a Christian is, of course, eternal life with Christ. We have not only received mercy and grace and had our sins forgiven, but so much more.

Why then do we meet people who have received Christ as their Savior and Lord who still seem unhappy? This is not right. There are troubles in this world, but with Jesus, we can have abundant life with Him. Abundant life is not a life free from pain, but with faith in Him, it is a way to live confident that He is working all things for our good.

Some Christians are still struggling along in life as if they didn't have a Father, Lord, and Savior who loves them and wants the best for them. They continue to live as they did before and do not enjoy His great love and the fruit of His Holy Spirit in their lives.

Of King David: Bless the Lord, O my soul, and all that is within me, bless his holy name! Bless the Lord, O my soul, and forget not all his benefits, who forgives all your iniquity, who heals all your diseases, who redeems your life from the pit, who crowns you with steadfast love and mercy, who satisfies you with good so that your youth is renewed like the eagles (Psalm 103:1-5).

The benefits of being a Christian are not just eternal. If we give Him our lives, our love, our worries, our cares, our joys, and hurts, we will have peace that passes our understanding. We can bring to God everything we have, everything we do and everything we think. He wants to have a personal relationship with us, closer than any personal relationship we have here, but if we spend less time with God than we do our human friends, we are missing out on many benefits.

He is the only friend who gives back to us more than we give, listens without complaining, and is always with us no matter what. God will bless us if we simply give ourselves to Him and to others. If we feel we are not receiving from God, perhaps it is because we are not giving to God.

> **If you then, who are evil, know how to give good gifts to your children, how much more will your Father who is in heaven give good things to those who ask him! (Matthew 7:11).**

Many people think that the world's misery is God's fault. Christians know that the powers of darkness at work in this world are truly the cause. God does not tempt us, nor does He cause bad things to happen.

We can't expect God to undo the laws of nature when something bad is happening. We can, however, expect God to bring good out of the situation for those who love Him. God only gives good gifts to His children.

> **Be not be conformed to this world, but be transformed by the renewal of your mind, that by testing you may discern what is the will of God, what is good and acceptable and perfect (Romans 12:2).**

Our benefits, our blessings come when we stay in communication with God, stay close to Him and seek to do the next right thing according to the scriptures. If we continue to live the same way we were living before He saved us, nothing will change in our lives on earth.

When we stay close to God, reading His word and praying for knowledge and wisdom daily, we will trust Him, feel His love, and live life with a different attitude. We will experience life more abundantly and joyfully.

We can't be stagnated Christians who are not receiving all the benefits He wants to give us. We need to make Christ the center of our lives, not our jobs, money, cars, or even family. God is first.

Putting Him off in a corner and only calling on Him when we need help is an unfair relationship. We wouldn't like it if our children or friends did that to us.

God's word is clear on this. He desires first place in every part of our lives. Though He already knows everything, He wants us to tell Him what is going on in our lives. He wants to commune with us and be the center of our world. It is not too much to give to Him when we consider the blessings we get in return.

But seek first the kingdom of God and his righteousness, and all these things will be added to you (Matthew 6:33).

We came to Christ because we know He is the way to abundant life on earth, and eternal life with Him in heaven. Seeking God first is the way to receive all His blessings or benefits. We don't seek God for the blessings, but the blessings are a by-product of seeking Him and putting Him first. The biggest benefit of all is that God loves us and sent His son to die in our place.

Prayer: **Lord, help us put you first in all things, not for your blessings and benefits but because you deserve it. Thank you for forgiving our selfishness and for blessing us even though we don't deserve it. We want to keep you in the center of our lives, minds, and hearts. Amen.**

His Life Was Not Easy

> **For to us a child is born, to us a son is given; and the government shall be upon his shoulder, and his name shall be called Wonderful Counselor, Mighty God, Everlasting Father, Prince of Peace (Isaiah 9:6).**

If we think our lives are difficult, we need to think about Jesus' life before starting His ministry.

We all know that Jesus came as a baby born in a barn. He was born of Mary, a virgin, conceived by the Holy Spirit, which might make us think that life was not that much of a hardship for Him. These mysteries are difficult to understand, but we know from historical records that these events occurred.

The book of Isaiah was written at least 200 and possibly 400 years before Jesus was born and predicts His birth. God was preparing the people for this momentous event. His plan to bring us back into a right relationship depended on Christ dying on the Cross for our sins, and to do that, He had to arrive on earth.

He could have just popped on the scene when He was thirty and started His ministry. He didn't have to come as a baby. He is God, after all. We don't realize how important the birth of Christ is. We celebrate His birthday, but we don't realize that He could have come in any way.

After His birth, His life was not easy. He was born in a very difficult situation. His family was not wealthy. They were not royalty. He had to learn to walk and talk just like every baby.

The King at the time was so set on killing Him that he had all the baby boys under 2 years old killed. What a wicked and difficult time it was.

> **Then Herod, when he saw that he had been tricked by the wise men, became furious, and he sent and killed all the male children in Bethlehem and in all that region who were two years old or under, according to the time that he had ascertained from the wise men (Matthew 2:16).**

I'm sure His family experienced fear for His life. He had brothers and sisters. He played, worked, slept, was cold, hot, and tired. His entire life was difficult, just like ours. He had good times and bad, just like us.

Sometimes I think we skip right from His birth, to His ministry, to His death without any thought to what His actual upbringing and life might have been. This is one reason Christ came as a baby.

God loved us so much that He allowed Jesus to experience everything we experience and more. We complain when things in our lives get difficult. We sometimes even blame God, but He understands our struggles and pain because He suffered them, too.

Life in this world will always be a struggle, but Jesus showed us the way to live. He forgives our bad choices when we bring them to Him. He is in heaven now, and we will be with Him someday, living without pain and struggles, but we need to follow His life examples here.

We need to love God and love each other and give of ourselves for His glory at Christmas and always. We can celebrate His birth, death, and resurrection, but should remember His life and thank Him for His great love and sacrifice.

So now faith, hope, and love abide, these three; but the greatest of these is love (1 Corinthians 13:13).

Prayer: **Lord, thank you for coming to us as a baby and living a life of struggle just like we do. Thank you for understanding us, loving us, and forgiving our sins. Show us the way to live as you would have us live, loving you and each other, trusting you and demonstrating your love to all. Amen.**

Trust Can Be a Choice

Now faith is the assurance of things hoped for, the conviction of things not seen (Hebrews 11:1).

We put our faith and trust in God, knowing that the hope we have in Jesus will come to pass. In God's word, the original meaning of trust is very similar to the word used for 'putting your faith in.' We put our faith in God, and we trust Him even when He doesn't do things the way we would like.

Do we do that for others? When we put our faith and trust in someone, and they let us down, do we continue to trust them?

We've heard people say that trust, once lost, must be earned. We understand that if someone has been untrustworthy or unfaithful, and let us down many times, we would have difficulty trusting them again. However, when we lose trust or faith in someone, can they actually **earn** it back?

It seems that even when they are not doing anything wrong, we struggle to trust them and withhold our faith. This attitude does not encourage their trustworthiness. Why bother if we are never going to trust them anyway?

It is a perpetual cycle that only ends when we, who have lost faith, choose to trust again without reserve because the more we don't trust, the more we don't trust.

There are some things in life that we must earn, and there are some things freely given. Where does trust come in? Trust is necessary for loving relationships to flourish, yet it is so easy to lose. Trust is vital for love.

Love bears all things, believes all things, hopes all things, endures all things (1 Corinthians 13:7).

Love, faith, trust, hope, and forgiveness are all tied up together for the Christian. True love must have faith and trust, and since we all make mistakes, there must also be forgiveness. God not only forgives us, but He also forgets about the wrong we committed.

When someone we love lets us down or does something untrustworthy, instead of holding it against them until a time when we might or might not trust them again, choose love and choose to trust them now. Choose to have faith that the untrustworthy act will not happen again. Choose to trust and forgive.

> *Trust is both an emotional and logical act. Emotionally, it is where you expose your vulnerabilities to people, but believing they will not take advantage of your openness. Logically, it is where you have assessed the probabilities of gain and loss, calculating expected utility based on hard performance data, and concluded that the person in question will behave in a predictable manner. In practice, trust is a bit of both. I trust you because I have experienced your trustworthiness and because I have faith in human nature* (Changingminds.org).

Even though the definition from Changingminds.org says that, logically, we assess whether someone will let us down again before we can decide to trust them, a Christian's attitude is different, especially with those we love. If love believes all things, shouldn't we choose to trust in our loved ones even after they have let us down?

> **Then Peter came to Jesus and asked, "Lord, how many times shall I forgive my brother who sins against me? Up to seven times?" Jesus answered, "I tell you, not just seven times, but seventy times seven times!" (Matthew 18:21, 22).**

Hopefully, we all understand that this does not apply to physical or mental abuse, adultery, or constantly repeated sin. We are talking about mistakes and even sin that the person is sincerely sorry for and determined not to repeat just as we are when we go to the Lord.

None of us are perfect, and the world and the devil are working to make us fail Christ and fail each other. Christ forgives us, so we need to forgive each other and make a choice to trust.

We can't truly forgive someone and then hold a lack of trust over their heads. That is not love or forgiveness. Love, forgiveness, and trust go together and are a choice that we make, not something that is earned. Our human nature wants proven trust, but trust and faith are choices and are not subject to proof.

> **Jesus said to him, "Have you believed because you have**

seen me? Blessed are those who have not seen and yet have believed" (John 20:29).

Faith, trust, and belief in God are greater because we have not seen. Trust, therefore, in a person without being proven or earned, is also greater. Difficult, yes, impossible, no. When we are struggling to trust someone in our lives, we can count on God to help us and to know when to choose to trust and when to forgive and move on.

"Behold, I am the Lord, the God of all flesh. Is anything too hard for me?" (Jeremiah 32:27).

***Prayer:* Lord, help us choose to trust those who have let us down and to have faith that our trust is deserved. Help us to know when to have faith and when to move on from difficult situations. Keep our minds from worry and fear and keep love in our hearts always. Thank you, Lord. Amen.**

Self-Forgiveness

"And whenever you stand praying, forgive, if you have anything against anyone, so that your Father also who is in heaven may forgive you your trespasses" (Mark 11:25).

Forgiving what others have against us and forgiving ourselves is difficult. God loves us and forgives our sins if we confess them to Him and ask Him into our hearts. That forgiveness is powerful, and we are instructed to forgive others in the same way, including ourselves.

Many of us have had times in life where we knew we were not living the way God would like us to and had no regard for the consequences. Even those who have been Christians for many years, active in the church, taught Sunday school, and had a wonderful relationship with Christ as their savior might have a past of which they are ashamed.

When someone with a sinful past, or a Christian who has been secretly sinning, wakes up and accepts the Lord or makes their way back to become whom God wants, they will ask for God's forgiveness, and it will be given. We have that assurance. God will forgive our sins.

God's forgiveness is ultimately what is important, but many who have been forgiven by God will still cry out to Him every time they remember their sins. They will ask the Lord over and over for His forgiveness, knowing in their hearts that they only need to ask once. The shame and guilt are overwhelming. This re-asking for forgiveness can go on for years or even a lifetime.

The church teaches us repeatedly that God loves us and forgives our sins but there is a forgiveness that is not discussed very often. Sometimes God must reveal it to us.

It is not God's forgiveness we are missing; it is our own.

"No longer will they teach their neighbor, or say to one another, 'Know the Lord,' because they will all know me, from the least of them to the greatest," declares the Lord. "For I will forgive their wickedness and will remember their sins no more" (Hebrews 8:11).

We need to listen when God tells us that He forgives us and that our sins are no longer remembered by Him. Now is the time to forgive ourselves. He does not remember our sins so why do we?

Even though this is not taught often in church, it is very important to our relationship with God. Forgiving oneself is not easy. The devil, the accuser, will bring up the shame of sin repeatedly.

If we continue to feel unforgiven, even knowing that God has forgiven us will make it difficult to mature in our relationship with Christ. It will be difficult to do any good for the kingdom if we continue to feel unworthy of God's love. Not forgiving ourselves make us unsuccessful in whatever we try to do for the Lord.

The Bible says a lot about forgiveness, but does not address forgiving oneself specifically. However, in Acts 10:34 (NIV), Peter said, **"In truth I perceive that God shows no partiality."** We know we should forgive others, so if we don't forgive ourselves, we are showing partiality. God forgives those we would consider to be the 'worst' of sinners, and we know that we must forgive them, too. So why is it so difficult to forgive ourselves?

God has forgiven us, and who are we to argue with God? To continually dwell on sins that God has forgiven is in direct opposition to what God tells us to do.

> ***Prayer:*** **Lord, thank you for forgiving my sins. I know that I must also forgive myself. Please help me to forgive myself for my behaviors, words, attitudes and all that I have done that was against your ways and help them not to come to my mind again. Amen.**

Joy:
The second fruit of the Holy Spirit

But the fruit of the Spirit is love, joy, peace, patience, kindness, goodness, faithfulness, gentleness, and self-control. Against such things there is no Law. And those who belong to Christ Jesus have crucified the flesh with its passions and desires. If we live by the Spirit, let us also keep in step with the Spirit (Galatians 5:22-25).

There are a few different biblical words used in both the Old and New Testaments that translate into 'joy.' The most common definition and listed as a synonym for these words is 'to rejoice.' Fellowship and relationship with God cause joy in believers.

In thy presence is fullness of joy; in thy right hand there are pleasures for evermore (Psalms 16:11).

God's presence gives us joy and His gift of Jesus Christ causes us to rejoice. He is joy, and He gives joy. He gives believers a joyous sense of security in life.

Knowing we have salvation and eternal life brings joy. Joy in the Lord is sometimes less of an emotion and more of an attitude. We know that God is in control and is working in our lives.

I hear, and my body trembles; my lips quiver at the sound; rottenness enters into my bones; my legs tremble beneath me. Yet I will quietly wait for the day of trouble to come upon people who invade us. Though the fig tree should not blossom, nor fruit be on the vines, the produce of the olive fail and the fields yield no food, the flock be cut off from the fold and there be no herd in the stalls, yet I will rejoice in the Lord; I will take joy in the God of my salvation (Habakkuk 3:16-18).

The God of Joy

He was in the world, and the world was made through him, yet the world did not know him (John 1:10).

The world does not know Christ, and each generation seems more selfish than the last. It is sad to see what a self-focused people we have become. People want what they want when they want it, and everything is at fast speed and posted on social media. People take more pictures of themselves than they do of anything else.

Being happy is the only goal in life these days, and everything humanity does is to reach that end. Seeking only our wants and needs is no longer looked down upon as selfishness, but as something we deserve. This behavior is celebrated as the way to be 'happy.'

We are seeking happiness and self-fulfillment, but we are looking in the wrong places for the wrong things. The God of joy is whom we should be seeking.

Though happiness is what everyone is seeking, the world is more and more unhappy with each passing day. If we look at past generations, we will see that they were happy at times, but they understood that it was a by-product of living a good life, doing good for others, and committing their lives to the service of the God of joy.

They realized that happiness was fleeting. Their care and concern for each other were more important than their own happiness. A greater percentage of people loved the Lord and had joy.

Rejoice in the Lord always; again I will say, Rejoice (Philippians 4:4).

The word *joy* in the Bible is closer in its definition to the word *rejoice*. Rejoicing is an attitude and a choice. We can choose to rejoice in all things even when we are not happy. God is in control, and that is the certainty we have that all will be well, and that brings rejoicing and joy. We trust the God of joy.

Studies have shown that the search for happiness has only resulted in misery and more seeking, without success. They show that 83% of Americans agree with this lifestyle of seeking our own happiness above all else (Yankelovich, James Davison Hunter) and, horror of horrors, many of these are young Christians. Instead of being driven by Christ's example of self-sacrifice, our own desires for happiness drive us.

> **Do not love the world or the things in the world. If anyone loves the world, the love of the Father is not in him. For all that is in the world—the desires of the flesh and the desires of the eyes and pride in possessions—is not from the Father but is from the world. And the world is passing away along with its desires, but whoever does the will of God abides forever (1 John 2:15-17).**

We love the things of the world, but the world does not teach us to do the will of God to attain joy. The sins that fall into three categories as listed in 1 John is what most people are doing to become 'happy', and these sins do not please the God of joy.

The world seeks the desires of the flesh, which are not only sex, but food, excessive exercise, dieting, drinking, drugs, and all the other things that please our bodies.

The desires of the eyes involve desiring or coveting what we see, i.e., new cars, clothes, someone else's husband or wife, all the wonderful things people post on Facebook. In Christianity, this would be considered covetousness, idolatry, and greed.

In some Bible versions, pride of possessions is the pride of life. Being proud because we own more than others or any pride that puts people, places or things above Christ or makes us feel we are equal to God is the same sin that Satan committed before he was cast from heaven. Many seek after honor and glory in their pride. Pride only brings destruction.

> **Now he told a parable to those who were invited, when he noticed how they chose the places of honor, saying to them, "When you are invited by someone to a wedding feast, do not sit down in a place of honor, lest someone more distinguished than you be invited by him, and he who invited you both will come and say to you, 'Give your place to this person,' and then you will begin with shame to take the lowest place. But when you are invited, go and sit in the**

lowest place, so that when your host comes he may say to you, 'Friend, move up higher.' Then you will be honored in the presence of all who sit at table with you. For everyone who exalts himself will be humbled, and he who humbles himself will be exalted" (Luke 14:7-11).

Humbling ourselves pleases the God of joy, and we will be exalted. Seeking happiness is an empty pursuit and is unsuccessful. Seeking happiness in the world is sin and does not produce the joy of the Lord.

We are different from the world. We must be humble and loving. We must stand firm, living as Christ lived, which is in self-sacrifice, not self-fulfillment, in seeking joy, not happiness.

For the kingdom of God is not a matter of eating and drinking but of righteousness and peace and joy in the Holy Spirit (Romans 14:17).

Prayer: **Lord, let us always choose joy over happiness in this world. We know that your joy strengthens us so that we can do the work that you would have us do. Help us to love those who seek only their happiness, and give us the ability to show them the difference between happiness and joy. Take all selfishness from us and replace it with your love for all. Amen.**

Just as We Are

But the Lord said to Samuel, "Do not look on his appearance or on the height of his stature, ... For the Lord sees not as man sees: man looks on the outward appearance, but the Lord looks on the heart" (1 Samuel 16:7).

God is looking at our hearts. Many of us feel unworthy to come to God. We think He will reject us because of the choices we have made and the lives we have lived. In our hearts, we want to believe that He loves us, but feel it can't be true. These feelings steal our joy, but God does not see us as we see ourselves.

The truth is that if our hearts turn to God and we believe that Jesus, His son, died in our place for our sins, we are worthy. God sees our hearts and wants us just as we are.

Picture a courtroom where the devil accuses us of committing all manner of sin. We are in filthy rags, ashamed to raise our eyes to the judge. We know that what we are accused of is true and we deserve to die. We have no defense. We made those choices, and we are unworthy to live.

But Jesus goes up to the judge and says, "I will die in their place. Yes, I know what they have done. I know all of it. Yes, I know some are murderers, thieves, drunkards, and the like, but they are my children, I love them, and I will die in their place if they let me."

The judge says "Okay" and turns to ask us if we will accept this amazing gift. We all say "Yes" with tears in our eyes, wondering why He would do such a thing for us.

Jesus is put to death, and not just any death, but a horrible, painful death, nailed hand and foot to the cross, bleeding and struggling to breathe.

Then a miraculous thing happens. Suddenly, we are in the finest robes of white. Everything we have ever done is gone, off the books. We are worthy to stand before God, and we hear Jesus say, "It is finished." We rejoice with the greatest joy ever felt.

The truth today is that as sinners, we are unworthy, but He is calling us to come just as we are so that we can say "yes, we accept this gift." We are now just as worthy as anyone who came before. Jesus loves us just as we are and is waiting for us to say "yes" to Him. He knows every bad choice and every sin of every kind that we have committed. He will forgive. Oh, what great joy!

> **Are not two sparrows sold for a penny? And not one of them will fall to the ground apart from your Father. But even the hairs of your head are all numbered. Fear not, therefore; you are of more value than many sparrows (Matthew 10:29-31).**

We are children of God once we accept His gift. We are no longer in filthy rags but are washed as white as snow.

Now that we are accepted as we are, we can walk with Jesus and bring others into His Kingdom. We can tell those who feel unworthy that they are loved. We can turn their heartache into joy.

> **Therefore, if anyone is in Christ, he is a new creation. The old has passed away; behold, the new has come (2 Corinthians 5:17).**

There is a beautiful old hymn that says it all: **Just As I Am:**

> *Just as I am, without one plea,*
> *But that Thy blood was shed for me,*
> *And that Thou bid'st me come to Thee,*
> *O Lamb of God, I come! I come!*

We need to hear Him with our hearts. He wants us to come now, just as we are. We are made worthy by accepting His gift. If we have asked Him into our hearts already, we are worthy. We must stop going back to the courtroom now because Jesus said, "It is finished." Learn to live in the joy of the redeemed.

> *Prayer:* **Lord, thank you for calling us to you just as we are. Help us to stop listening to the accuser tell us that we are unworthy. Don't let us wait, thinking we must be better before we can come to you. Jesus, you rose from the dead so we can have eternal life with you. Let us rejoice now, knowing that your death makes us worthy. Amen**

Focused on Christ Crucified

> **And I am convinced that nothing can ever separate us from God's love. Neither death nor life, neither angels nor demons, neither our fears for today nor our worries about tomorrow—not even the powers of hell can separate us from God's love. No power in the sky above or in the earth below—indeed, nothing in all creation will ever be able to separate us from the love of God that is revealed in Christ Jesus our Lord (Romans 8:38-39).**

What great joy we have knowing that nothing can separate us from God's love. But do we understand that we can separate our love from Him? We can allow ourselves distractions through ideas that seem religious in nature, taking our focus from Him.

As Christians, we may become interested in things that mask themselves as pertaining to Christ. Studies and discussions of topics in the spiritual world can draw us away from our focus on the basic salvation message. Gradually we become so involved in attaining so-called knowledge that our joy in life is gone because we have not remained focused on Christ, His crucifixion, and resurrection.

These studies and discussions may seem that they are helping us focus on God. The devil loves to get our minds on religious questions and discussions that move God out of the center of our lives and make us think we are seeking religious knowledge.

As Christians, we try to balance this life and keep our focus on Christ so that we can show others the joy He brings. When we get out of balance by focusing on vain religious discussions instead of Christ's death and resurrection, we will not be able to show His joy.

> **O Timothy, guard the deposit entrusted to you. Avoid the irreverent babble and contradictions of what is falsely called 'knowledge' (1 Timothy 6:20).**

Many Christians enjoy research and study of religious knowledge or worldly politics. There are many books on subjects like the Illuminati, casting out demons, the rapture, the antichrist, and the second coming. There is nothing wrong with studying or researching these topics and others like them if they don't take our focus off the joy of salvation.

Time reading the word of God is very important, especially when studying other things. It is when these studies and discussions take precedence over God's Word that we get into trouble.

Often it is those who want more, i.e., the new Christian, enthusiastic youth, or the fainthearted (those who struggle with their faith) that become interested in topics that are not about the Good News. They can become so focused on these that they forget about their personal relationship with Jesus and still think they are doing something good.

We are so convinced that we are doing the work of God by delving deeply into these subjects that we forget to read about and dwell on God's love and His plan for our lives. Then we wonder why we are not experiencing the joy that God provided by His Holy Spirit.

> **But avoid foolish controversies, genealogies, dissensions, and quarrels about the law, for they are unprofitable and worthless (Titus 3:9).**

Arguments and lengthy religious discussions that aren't about His love and salvation can cause strife and anger when God wants joy and peace. Many of these issues are very interesting, and the subjects seem right up our religious alley. This danger is mentioned many times in the Bible.

Mathew Henry says, "Mere talk, especially in religion, is meaningless, and yet many people's religion consists of little else but meaningless talk."

What we should study and focus on is how to bring the lost into God's kingdom. God wants His love, joy, plan of salvation, and following the example of Christ to be central. We have been sent out into the world to save others.

Each day, we should spend time bringing ourselves back to the simple truth that Jesus loves us and died for our sins. We must confess our sins and keep Christ at the center of our minds, worshiping Him and building a relationship with Him.

> **Have nothing to do with irreverent, silly myths. Rather**

train yourself for godliness; for while bodily training is of some value, godliness is of value in every way, as it holds promise for the present life and also for the life to come (1 Timothy 4:7-8).

The devil is a liar and uses every means available to draw our love away from Christ because He knows He can never draw Christ's love away from us. Knowing that he uses the study of biblical topics and topics about him, we are more careful what we chose to study and how much we will become involved in vain discussions.

Certain persons, by swerving from these, have wandered away into vain discussions, desiring to be teachers of the law, without understanding what they are saying (1 Timothy 1:6-7).

We are responsible for protecting our relationship with Christ so we can experience the joy He has for us and show it to the world. We don't want to wander or be drawn away from our focus.

***Prayer:* Lord, while we are studying religious topics of interest, please let us always come back to love, praise and worship you. We want to always experience the joy you want us to have, not the stress of debate or the deep concentration of study that takes us away from you. We thank you, Jesus, for forgiving our sins and dying on the cross so that we could have eternal life. Help us remember to keep you in the center of our lives and to talk to you daily. Amen.**

Tiny Church

> **Shepherd the flock of God that is among you, exercising oversight, not under compulsion, but willingly, as God would have you; not for shameful gain, but eagerly; not domineering over those in your charge, but being examples to the flock (1 Peter 5:2-3).**

Tiny houses are very popular these days, but what is a tiny church? Our families could be considered tiny churches. Parents are the pastors, and children and other people living in the household are the congregation. Let's think about this.

We are the church of God, and not just when we are in the church building. Our families can enjoy every day being the flock of our tiny church at home.

The church and its pastor offer many benefits for the congregation such as instruction, prayer, encouragement, advice, joyful worship, comfort, and admonishment. Parents can do the same.

There is a lot of information out there about how to be a good parent and have a happy home. Some of it is valuable, but they don't talk about parents or guardians as shepherds over the flock of Christ, which is what we are. The church provides prayer and encouragement, but inside our own families, we just 'wing it' even though our families are of great importance to us.

In thinking about church, we know that there are Bible studies, classes, music programs, camping, and lots of eating. We probably do most of these in our homes, but they are not always joyful and focused on Christ. If we were to model our homes after the church, we would talk to our families about God, sing Christian songs, worship, pray, and thank God for all our blessings.

When we go camping or on other adventures, Christ would always be a part of the activity. As Christian parents, we know that it is important to encourage, give advice, comfort, and admonish, but is Christ the center of these conversations?

Regarding the Christians that Peter was teaching, Paul told him to shepherd the flock. He could have been speaking to us about our families. We should oversee our children and those in our care out of love, eagerly, and not in a domineering, controlling way, but as examples. There isn't any 'do as I say, not as I do' in the family church. We want to have joy in our home life, and this is one way God has provided for us.

This scripture has instructions for pastors of churches and for parents, comparing them to shepherds. Shepherds love their sheep and take great care of their health and well-being. The sheep know the shepherd and trust him. The shepherds willingly watch over the sheep.

As a member of a family unit or as a sheep, we can be like members of the church, faithful and constantly learning and growing.

> **Train up a child in the way he should go; even when he is old he will not depart from it (Proverbs 22:6).**

We want our families to serve God, have joy, and live long and productive lives. If we start to think of ourselves as pastors of a tiny church in everything we do, we might find that we must do some things differently.

It is the pastor of the church or the leader of the family unit who teaches the members the joy of knowing the Lord. If we want our children to accept Jesus as their Lord and Savior, then we must share and show them the way to salvation through Christ.

As sheep, we are willing to learn from our parents or guardians so that we can grow up as God wants, becoming God-centered and not self-centered.

> **Fathers, do not provoke your children to anger, but bring them up in the discipline and instruction of the Lord (Ephesians 6:4).**

If, as parents, we think of ourselves as pastors of our tiny church we will consider the effect that our actions and reactions have on the sheep. If we can do that, our mini congregations will grow in knowledge and love of the Lord, and our homes will fill with joy, which is our hope and prayer. Our family is our church of God.

> **Pay careful attention to yourselves and to all the flock, in which the Holy Spirit has made you overseers, to care for the church of God, which he obtained with his own blood (Acts 20:28).**

If our family members see a different person attending church on Sunday from the person they live with at home, we are grieving the Holy Spirit. Jesus gave His blood for our lives and our churches. Pray that we don't leave church at church but take it all to our tiny church at home.

Prayer: **Lord, let us follow your example in all things, no matter if we are the shepherd of our home or a follower. We want to serve you, Lord, learn about you and have a close relationship with you so that our lives will be filled with your joy. Amen.**

Lost Hope

Why are you in despair, oh my soul? And why are you disturbed within me? Hope in God, for I shall again praise Him, my countenance and my God (Psalms 43:5).

Our hope is in God. Without hope, life is desolate. When we have nothing to hope for, despair can overwhelm us. When things fall apart, we can lose hope in an instant, believing that it will never be good again. We can lose hope in friendships. We can lose hope of ever finding love or of ever getting a job.

Every day, we hope for something, or we lose hope in something. Most lost hope is temporary, but when you are in the midst, it feels permanent.

But hope is somewhat different for the Christian. Our modern worldly definition of hope is to wish for something, but without certainty. In scripture, according to both the Hebrew and the Greek, 'Hope' is a strong and confident expectation. This implies a certainty that when our hope is in God, He will do as He has promised.

May the God of hope fill you with all joy and peace in believing, so that by the power of the Holy Spirit you may abound in hope (Romans 15:13).

Believing in God with a strong and confident expectation will fill us with joy. Both the worldly and the scriptural definitions can apply to our daily lives. When we hope we will get a job or that someone will call us, we don't have a certainty that either of those things will happen because they are worldly hopes.

When we have hope in God, we have joy because we know He is working for our good. When we wait on Him, He will give what we need and what is best for us in the proper time, and we can rejoice while we wait to see what God has in store for us.

When we feel that we have nothing to hope for, we can remind ourselves that we do have hope in God and the assurance that He is and will continue to bless us with what we need.

For in hope we have been saved, but hope that is seen is not

hope; for why does one also hope for what he sees? But if few hope for what we do not see, with perseverance we wait eagerly for it (Romans 8:24-25).

Often, we confuse wanting with hope. We become discouraged when things do not go the way we want them to. We lose hope. Wanting is not the same as hope, and God does not always give us what we want.

Today we must decide to wait on what God is planning for us, whether it is what we want or not. Our lives are in His hands, and it does us no good to fret and worry about it. God is the same yesterday, today and forever. We can rejoice in Him no matter what the world throws at us. The joy of the Lord gives us strength.

Prayer: **Dear Heavenly Father, we hope in You. Your plans for us are better than we could ever hope for in this world. Help us not to become discouraged or frustrated when the world lets us down. We ask for more faith in all things. We trust in you. Amen.**

God Is Looking Out for Us

Be strong and courageous. Do not fear or be in dread of them, for it is the Lord your God who goes with you. He will not leave you or forsake you (Deuteronomy 31:6).

Fear is a human reaction, usually to present events or something perceived to be coming. Fear is sometimes a catalyst to a positive action, but to what action should fear always propel us?

Fear, if we trust in God, can bring us joy. By knowing that the Lord our God goes with us, we can look forward to seeing what He will do. We can strive to be strong and courageous waiting for the miracles that God will work in our lives during difficult situations.

We may feel like we are being thrown to the lions, but we haven't, and even if we were, we would come out just fine.

We are God's children. When you bring a child into this world, you are responsible for looking out for them, and this is even more true with God, our creator. If mothers feel that way about their children, how much more does God feel that way about us?

If our fear is that God will not produce the results we are looking for, we know that this fear is wrong. This is a trick of the devil, who wants to paralyze us with fear instead of allowing us to have an attitude of rejoicing, no matter what the circumstances. God will produce the results that we need.

In this world, bad things will happen, but to know that God is looking out for us can give peace that we cannot fully understand. What should fear produce in us if we know that God is looking out for us? The answer again is joy.

"Therefore I tell you, do not be anxious about your life, what you will eat or what you will drink, nor about your body, what you will put on. Is not life more than food, and the body more than clothing? Look at the birds of the air: they neither sow nor reap nor gather into barns, and yet your heavenly Father feeds them. Are you not of more value than they? And which of you by being anxious can add a single hour to his span of life? And why are you anxious about clothing? Consider the lilies of the field, how they

grow: they neither toil nor spin, yet I tell you, even Solomon in all his glory was not arrayed like one of these" (Matthew 6:25-34).

We can have joy knowing there is a plan for our lives, no matter what we do to mess things up. We can have joy about current issues, knowing that God is working in everyone's lives and wants all to come into His kingdom. We can act positively when we are afraid, preparing the best we can and leaving the rest to God. Letting fear stop us from living as we should is not God's will for us.

The Lord your God is in your midst, a mighty one who will save; he will rejoice over you with gladness; he will quiet you by his love; he will exult over you with loud singing (Zephaniah 3:17).

It would be naïve to think that nothing bad will ever happen, but to live in fear is a lack of trust in God. God is looking out for us. We are His children, and although terrible things happen in this world, with God's help, we can trust in Him and react with a certainty that He is in control.

Prayer: **Lord, quiet our fears with your joy. Remind us that you are with us even when we are afraid and that you will allow what is best for us. Help us to give up our worrying and strife to you, leaving it at your feet and trusting in your loving goodness. We know you are looking out for us. Amen.**

After Bad Decisions

> **For though we walk in the flesh, we are not waging war according to the flesh. For the weapons of our warfare are not of the flesh but have divine power to destroy strongholds. We destroy arguments and every lofty opinion raised against the knowledge of God, and take every thought captive to obey Christ (2 Corinthians 10:3-5).**

We are at war, and it often causes us to make bad choices in life. We are fallible human beings living in a sinful, evil world. We make decisions that we think are right, and later, we may discover that we have made a serious mistake, have failed God, have broken a vow or the law. We start to beat ourselves up.

Satan, the accuser, points his finger and tells us that we are terrible and perhaps stupid to have made such a decision and that we should hang our heads in shame. He will do anything in his limited power to draw us away from God and make us think that we are unworthy of God's love. He wants to steal our joy and make us forget about God's great forgiveness.

We have been given the weapons to fight against this accuser and win. We have the Holy Spirit and the assurance that we have been forgiven if we confess our sins to our Father in heaven. Bad choices and bad decisions, even with selfish motives, are not only forgiven but forgotten when we bring them to God. We must forgive ourselves too, ignoring the accuser and listening only to God to have the joy He wants us to have.

Clearly, God understands what we are fighting against and that we make decisions based on the information available to us. We also make decisions based on our own selfish desires, sometimes out of anger and sometimes out of fear or other emotions.

Even though we have help from God to fight this war and make better decisions, there are times when we still go our own way. If we don't mature as Christians, we will live in a state of shame, guilt and feeling unworthy.

We know that God has provided forgiveness for our bad choices. We know about His love and His joy, so if we continue to live in our shame, we are ignoring God's provisions for us. We have laid down the weapons He has given to us to destroy the devil.

When we ask God for wisdom and knowledge to help us mature as Christians, we have assurance that He has forgiven our pasts and that His Holy Spirit is with us and will teach us. He will give us knowledge, and the wisdom to use that knowledge, to follow Christ's example. His joy will be ours.

We all face trials and temptations. We all make bad decisions. God forgives us, and we need to forgive ourselves.

> **Count it all joy, my brothers, when you meet trials of various kinds, for you know that the testing of your faith produces steadfastness. And let steadfastness have its full effect, that you may be perfect and complete, lacking in nothing (James 1:2-4).**

Steadfastness comes with Christian maturity. Christian maturity comes from having a close relationship with God, continued prayer and studying the word of God. Then comes the joy of knowing God's love even after we've made bad decisions.

> **You have turned my mourning into joyful dancing. You have taken away my clothes of mourning and clothed me with joy (Psalms 30:11).**

Trusting God brings joy, not mourning. Our lives and our futures are in His hands. He will make us dance with joy and take away our sadness.

> **May the God of hope fill you with all joy and peace in believing, so that by the power of the Holy Spirit you may abound in hope (Romans 15:13).**

> *Prayer:* **Lord, it is difficult to forgive ourselves for bad decisions. Help us, each time our sins come to mind, to remember that you have forgiven us. Give us the joy of having you in our hearts, leading and guiding us as we mature and draw closer to you. Amen.**

What Does Joy Feel Like?

For to set the mind on the flesh is death, but to set the mind on the Spirit is life and peace (Romans 8:6).

Joy sometimes feels like happiness. Joy sometimes doesn't feel like anything. Joy is not always an emotion. It is sometimes an attitude, a choice, a decision. It is the assurance that God is in control. Setting our minds on the Holy Spirit is choosing to rejoice, and that brings life and peace.

Joy can manifest itself as contentment or a certain calmness. It is the assurance that all is well with our souls and a determination to have faith when all around us is seemingly falling apart.

Outwardly, when things are obviously bad, and people around us are aware of our struggles, our choice to have joy from the Lord witnesses to them. The apostles were able to show joy even in chains. Were they feeling joy, or did they choose to rejoice?

They knew without a doubt that they were where God wanted them. They knew that their suffering meant that they were doing something right for God, and the world hated them. It was exactly as it should have been. That certainty is what joy feels like.

For thus said the Lord God, the Holy One of Israel, "In returning and rest you shall be saved; in quietness and in trust shall be your strength" (Isaiah 30:15).

When we think we have nothing to look forward to and our prayers seem to go unanswered, our faith may waiver. Quietness and trust shall be our strength. We know that God is still there, and that life doesn't always go smoothly.

Waiting on the Lord to make us happy is not the way to joy. Joy is a fruit of the Holy Spirit that we can seek, remembering that joy is not always a feeling but an attitude of trust.

Our feelings of joy may slip away, but we can't let our determination to rejoice be lost. Continuing to cry out to God and ask 'why?' is understandable and can even be helpful as we grow in faith. The more we communicate with God and share our burdens with other Christians, despite not feeling joy, the feelings of contentment and faith will strengthen, and that is joy.

Joy is an emotion, but it is also an attitude, a choice, an inner certainty, or even a hope that grows into certainty as we mature in the knowledge of Christ.

For we walk by faith, not by sight (2 Corinthians 5:7).

Beginning this journey of accepting that joy, that is not always felt, is difficult. All of our wondering, waiting, wishing, and wanting can grow into the inner faith that produces joy. Continuing with God as the center of our lives will bear this fruit.

Prayer: **Lord, let us choose joy over fear and worry. Give us the calm assurance that you are in control and everything will be as you want. Lift our hearts as we choose joy because we are an emotional people. And help us show your joy to all the world no matter what is happening. Amen.**

Peace:
The third fruit of the Holy Spirit

But the fruit of the Spirit is love, joy, peace, patience, kindness, goodness, faithfulness, gentleness, and self-control. Against such things there is no Law. And those who belong to Christ Jesus have crucified the flesh with its passions and desires. If we live by the Spirit, let us also keep in step with the Spirit (Galatians 5:22-25).

Peace with God comes from His grace and from His provision of salvation through Jesus Christ. Jesus in our hearts gives us peace that we cannot comprehend.

The word *peace* comes from the Greek word **eireinei** and is used in two ways. It means the tranquility that we have once we have a relationship with God.

Therefore, being justified by faith, we have peace with God through our Lord Jesus Christ (Romans 5:1).

It is also the mental peace of God we can have daily when living as believers.

For God has not given us a spirit of fear; but of power, and of love, and of a sound mind (2 Timothy 1:7).

There are two ways for us to have the peace of God. First, through our salvation, and daily as we live a Christian life, content with what we have and building our personal relationship with God.

You keep him in perfect peace, whose mind is stayed on thee; because he trusts in you (Isaiah 26:3-4).

The God of Peace

Now may the Lord of peace himself give you peace at all times in every way. The Lord be with you all (2 Thessalonians 3:16).

We all want to live peaceful lives at all times and in every way. We want peace from our anxieties, in our families, with our spouse, in our jobs, between political parties, between people of different beliefs and cultures, and between nations. In this world, peace does not reign. We are not naturally a peaceful people.

Even those of the world who say they want peace are sometimes not peaceful in trying to attain it. It is impossible to bring peace when there is no peace in our hearts. Peace in our hearts only comes from God, so it is impossible for unbelievers to have real peace, live in peace, or to bring peace to the world.

You keep him in perfect peace whose mind is stayed on you, because he trusts in you (Isaiah 26:3).

Perfect peace comes from believing and trusting that God is working on our behalf in this sinful world. We can have peace in our hearts and in our families if God is the center of our lives. We may struggle at times with anxiety and fear, not trusting that our Father will care for us. When we feel anxious, we must reign in those doubts and remember that God is over our lives. We are not of the world.

We will have trouble in this life. Bad things will happen to believers as well as those who don't believe. Human nature dictates that we will have disagreements even at church. This does not mean there is no peace. With right hearts, we can disagree and still have peace and love for our brothers and sisters in the Lord.

If possible, so far as it depends on you, live peaceably with all (Romans 12:18).

As far as it depends on us, Paul said in Romans, we should live in peace. Lack of peace resides where there is pride, confusion, and in those whose minds are not on building each other up. If we were to go after peace like we go after the other desires of our hearts, each of us would have joy, and together we would show God to the world.

We can seek peace and receive it by believing that God will meet our needs, by guarding our hearts and minds against evil, and by knowing that we are of great value to Him. Believing and trusting come from reading God's word and learning not to be anxious about our lives.

We can, as far as it depends on us, live in peace in the world by turning away from evil and doing good for the Lord. We must strive to live a righteous life and draw on God's strength through His Holy Spirit in all situations.

> **For the kingdom of God is not a matter of eating and drinking but of righteousness and peace and joy in the Holy Spirit (Romans 14:17).**

Those who have not put their faith in God and have not accepted Christ as their Lord and Savior will never have true peace. Peace and joy only come from God. There is peace for a time among nonbelievers, but in the end, their selfish desires will drive the peace away.

We cannot repay evil for evil, or delight in our own desires. We must humble ourselves and determine in our hearts not to be anxious about life and what it will bring. We must uplift each other and not try to put ourselves in the highest places. We must not take vengeance against each other or hold grudges. We cannot live like unbelievers. There is no peace there.

A life with hardships is better with peace than a life with everything we want that is full of strife.

> **I have said these things to you, that in me you may have peace. In the world you will have tribulation. But take heart; I have overcome the world (John 16:33).**

> *Prayer:* **Lord, we know that to have peace around us, we must have you in our hearts. We must trust in your ways and your plans. We must not repay evil with evil. Help us to control our human nature and allow your nature to flow through us. Help us to bring peace to all those around us and show them you, the God of peace. Amen.**

God Hears You

The Lord is far from the wicked, but he hears the prayer of the righteous (Proverbs 15:29).

God hears us when we talk with Him as if we were the only one speaking. He is not some far off God who set us here and now just waits to see what happens. He is our father. He loves us, and He wants us to have abundant life as His children.

He is everywhere. He knows all things, sees all things, and lives in the hearts of those who worship Him. There is no place that we can go where God is not there. There is nothing we do that God does not see. There is never a time when God does not hear us. Daily peace comes from knowing He is always near.

We know that we are not perfect and may even feel wicked, but God sees our hearts, and He loves us. When we come to Him for forgiveness, He forgives. When we come with needs, He will meet those needs. He knows what we really need, and He is working in our lives to make us better people, better Christians, and better witnesses for him. He wants us to have joy, love, and peace. He wants us to talk to Him.

The eyes of the Lord are in every place, keeping watch on the evil and the good (Proverbs 15:3).

God is everywhere. When we talk to God or call on the Holy Spirit, He hears. When we pray, we are talking to our greatest friend. Talking with God does not require fancy speech. We do not need to use many words or big words. He knows what we need before we need it, but He wants us to bring those needs to Him. He likes to talk to us. He wants us to share our lives, seek His guidance, and confess our wrongdoings. He wants our love because He first loved us.

Let us then with confidence draw near to the throne of grace, that we may receive mercy and find grace to help in time of need (Hebrews 4:16).

We can draw near with confidence. We can talk to God about anything. He already knows everything. When we talk to Him, we know that He hears us, and He is not struggling to hear us above the crowd. To feel His peace, our communication is constant, bringing everything to Him during our days.

We don't understand Omnipotence, but God is, and because of that, He can hear only us when we pray. We have His full attention for as long, and as often, as we want, every one of us.

Even when we have sinned, we are confident that when we ask forgiveness of God, He will give it, and give His peace with it. Christ died so that we might have that forgiveness.

Being truthful with God, no matter how difficult, is blessed by Him, and revealing our sins and weakness is such a relief. We are afraid of the truth because we don't want to lose His great mercy, grace, and forgiveness. But when we confess our sins and ask Him to forgive them, He does, and He wipes them from His memory.

Because of His death, we are in right relationship with the Father and confident that when we talk to Him, He is listening. We can bring everything to Him—worship, thankfulness, needs, wants, pain, and fear. He wants to discuss it all with us and fill our hearts with the peace of knowing that He is there and He cares.

I cried to him with my mouth, and high praise was on my tongue. If I had cherished iniquity in my heart, the Lord would not have listened. But truly God has listened; he has attended to the voice of my prayer. Blessed be God, because he has not rejected my prayer or removed his steadfast love from me! (Psalm 66:17-20).

Prayer: Thank you, Lord, for listening to us even when we are not saying the things you would like us to say. Thank you for the peace we have, knowing that you are with us every day, no matter where we are or what we are doing. Help us bring everything to you along with our worship and praise. Amen.

Break Every Chain

For God will break the chains that bind his people and the whip that scourges them, just as he did when he destroyed the vast host of the Midianites by Gideon's little band (Isaiah 9:4).

God will break the chains or strongholds of the negative things we struggle with. We have chains of fear of the future, anger, envy, addiction, immorality, impatience, self-doubt, self-righteousness, laziness, the inability to listen to others, and many other things.

Our past actions chain us, even though Christ has forgiven them. This life is a war, and we must arm ourselves with a closeness to God like never before, giving our strongholds to Him so He can free us from our chains.

We are struggling with our sinful nature, i.e., the spirit with which we were born (the old man). We will continue to fight these battles every day against the powers of darkness in this world. These powers are going all-out to chain us. When we become Christians, the evil in this world begins an all-out war against us.

For we wrestle not against flesh and blood, but against principalities, against powers, against the rulers of the darkness of this world, against spiritual wickedness in high places (Ephesians 6:12).

We must ask God and look deeply into our hearts to see what it is that has a stronghold on us. We cannot have peace while we are bound by the desires of this world. We are not fighting others. We are fighting Satan.

Sometimes just spending too much time thinking about our own problems is a stronghold. While we are thinking about ourselves, we can't think about others, we don't pray for them, and we don't help them.

The ideology of this world tells us to focus on ourselves, our wants, and our miseries, but focusing on ourselves can bring about a negative attitude which becomes a chain around our necks. Focusing on the negative does not bring peace. Anger and hatred leave no room for peace.

Do not be conformed to this world, but be transformed by the renewal of your mind, that by testing you may discern what is the will of God, what is good and acceptable and perfect (Romans 12:2).

This world is evil and getting worse. Non-Christians are blinded by this evil, which often masquerades as good, and they do not understand the ways of our God. They seek after peace, but they cannot find it because they don't know what true peace is. They want us to join them and will do anything in their power (TV shows, commercials, news, social media, alcohol, drugs, parties, groups, etc.) to chain and bind us to the things of the world.

The Holy Spirit was given to us as a helper. We are to ask for knowledge and wisdom so that we can walk according to God's will, even while we remain in the world. Knowledge and wisdom are not the same things. We obtain knowledge by learning about and discerning the things that chain us, and we use wisdom to make decisions and take actions that allow us to escape those bonds.

We must take steps to turn away from those strongholds and stop committing sins. We can't expect freedom from an alcohol addiction if we continue to spend time in bars. How can we be free of the chains of gambling if we continue to go to the casino? Wisdom tells us to turn from sin and that anything that controls us is sin. Changing our life patterns is one of the steps we must take so that God can work in us to break the chains.

We have an all-powerful God who will break our worldly chains if we ask Him. This is spiritual warfare, and God has given us Christ and the Holy Spirit as our weapons. God will win this war. Will we be part of His army or will we be chained up without hope and the ability to escape? Will we live in strife or will we live in peace?

Jesus answered them, "Truly, truly, I say to you, everyone who commits sin is a slave to sin. ...So if the Son sets you free, you will be free indeed" (John 8:34 and 36).

Prayer: **Lord, please show us our chains and then break them. We can't do it on our own. We want your peace and**

to live as you would have us live. Please give us wisdom to know what is holding us back and the knowledge to make the right decisions. Amen.

What are Christians Focusing On?

Finally, brothers, whatever is true, whatever is honorable, whatever is just, whatever is pure, whatever is lovely, whatever is commendable, if there is any excellence, if there is anything worthy of praise, think about these things (Philippians 4:8).

What is it that we are thinking about? Television, radio, Facebook, social media, movies, friends, co-workers, and other activities all go into our brains and stay there. Situations like finances, relationships, and illness fill our minds with worry and concern. Is there any room for God in there? Is there any room for peace?

In their case the god of this world has blinded the minds of the unbelievers, to keep them from seeing the light of the gospel of the glory of Christ, who is the image of God (2 Cor. 4:4).

The world is not a positive place. People with blinded eyes are turning every which way searching for the light of the gospel. They are protesting in the streets, fighting among themselves, and thinking of ways to destroy each other, the government, and anyone who doesn't think as they do. All they do is grab at things they think will make them happy. The more they seek happiness, the unhappier they become.

The world is lost, but we are not of the world, and we focus on Jesus Christ. How can we do this if our minds fill up with all the troubles of the world? We can't allow ourselves to be sucked in by the evil.

What are we focusing on daily? Are we as blinded by worldly things, letting them fill our minds, as nonbelievers? Is the world all we think about? Only when we focus on the things of God will we have peace. He takes care of worldly activities and stresses. When we bring our concerns before Him, He will work on our behalf. He is our Father.

If then you have been raised with Christ, seek the things that are above, where Christ is, seated at the right hand

> **of God. Set your minds on things that are above, not on things that are on earth (Col. 3:1,2).**

We are no longer of this world. We have been raised to new life in Christ. We must seek the things that are above. Balance is important in life. We must find a balance between being aware of what is going on in the world and getting so involved that we watch the news all day long in despair.

What we spend our time thinking about is what will rule us. We must set our minds on things that are above in heavenly places.

> **You keep him in perfect peace whose mind is stayed on you, because he trusts in you (Isaiah 26:3).**

When our minds are on the things of the Lord, our trust in Him grows, and with trust comes peace. Nonbelievers will look at us and wonder why we are so joyful with the world as it is. The happiness they seek is fleeting, but true joy and peace are eternal and are not dependent on people or things.

When God is in control of our lives, our peace will show others what we are focusing on. Our lives and our speech will show others *whom* we are focusing on. God has a plan for each of us if we continue to focus our attention on Him and not on the world.

> **If you were of the world, the world would love you as its own; but because you are not of the world, but I chose you out of the world, therefore the world hates you (John 15:19).**

> ***Prayer:*** **Lord, help us to remember that we are chosen out of the world, and we must keep our focus on Christ. We know that He will take care of us, no matter how evil things get in this world. Thank you for the peace of knowing that you are in control. Help us to stay the course. Amen.**

Being Satisfied

Not that I am speaking of being in need, for I have learned in whatever situation I am to be content (Philippians 4:11).

Whatever our situation, God wants us satisfied, but it seems that we are not an easily satisfied people. We want more things, better jobs, more respect, and an easier life. We are always striving for more in this world, even though we know we already have what is most important and that is salvation through Jesus Christ.

Satisfaction is a form of peace from the Lord. Being satisfied that we are where He wants us and are doing what He wants us to do brings rest from our struggles. We need to accept that God has chosen this time and this place for us. He has chosen our work, whom we work with, and what we have for this day.

We may believe that there is more out there for us to do. Sometimes we want to do more for God but feel stifled and stuck. If we take a breath and realize that not everything has to happen today or tomorrow, that God wants us here now at this moment, our lives will have more peace.

It is not that we don't want to plan or look forward to our future, but we can't let it frustrate or depress us while we wait. God will open doors in His time and in His way. It is fine for us to envision what we think might be a better future, as long as we accept that God's plan may differ.

We often ask God why life is so stressful, only to find that we are the ones who make it so by fretting and worrying about things out of our control. Our situation may not be ideal as the world views it, but we are satisfied where we are because our God is in control.

Now there is great gain in godliness with contentment, for we brought nothing into the world, and we cannot take anything out of the world. But if we have food and clothing, with these we will be content (1 Timothy 6:6-8).

We all want contentment, and we think that we will be more content if God will just give us what we ask for. But contentment comes from trusting God to lead us. When we are in difficulty, we ask it to be removed, but to be content if it is not removed is true satisfaction.

We all want what we don't have, but God wants us satisfied with what we have been given during those times so that we can wait on Him and see what great things He will do.

If we are always fretting about our lot in life, we will miss the marvelous things that God is doing all around us. We will not experience His strength or be upheld by His right hand because we are too busy complaining about what He hasn't done.

> **I know how to be brought low, and I know how to abound. In any and every circumstance, I have learned the secret of facing plenty and hunger, abundance and need. I can do all things through him who strengthens me (Philippians 4:12-13).**

Seeking only God and where He wants us is the key to peace and contentment. Being satisfied with what He provides and taking one day at a time will bring us joy. We must truly believe that God knows what He is doing, and we have only to continue to draw closer to Him to be satisfied in life.

The closer our relationship with God, the more He will lead us into greater work for Him. All else means nothing. Only what we do for Christ matters. He will always be with us, and we are to show Him to the world. If we are not satisfied with what God has provided, we cannot show how wonderful it is to know Him.

> **For the sake of Christ, then, I am content with weaknesses, insults, hardships, persecutions, and calamities. For when I am weak, then I am strong (2 Corinthians 12:10).**

> ***Prayer:*** **Lord Jesus, help us be satisfied with what you have provided and where you have placed us. Let us draw closer to you daily and ask only what we can do for you. If our lives are difficult, let us be content while you make us stronger. Help us to take the steps that you lead us to take, showing the world how great your loving kindness is to us all. Amen.**

God Keeps His Promises

By which he has granted to us his precious and very great promises, so that through them you may become partakers of the divine nature, having escaped from the corruption that is in the world because of sinful desire (1 Peter 1:4).

There are 5,467 promises of God in the Bible. Many of His promises are about the birth of Jesus and His death and resurrection. These promises of God were all fulfilled.

Many of His promises are for us so that we know His loving care and commitment to bringing everyone to salvation through Christ.

There are promises about the gift of the Holy Spirit to the Apostles, abundant life, eternal life, the forgiveness of sins, peace, joy, and so much more. Anytime we are struggling or just want a promise to hang on to, we can look them up in God's word. In today's world, all we need is to place our question on the Internet. We can google "what does the Bible say about____?" It couldn't be easier to know the promises of God.

Since we have these promises, beloved, let us cleanse ourselves from every defilement of body and spirit, bringing holiness to completion in the fear of God (2 Corinthians 7:1).

When someone promises something, we expect it done. We count on it as if it is already completed because it was promised. God never goes back on His promises. What He has said, we can count on as completed.

God promises He is with us always and in every place, even when we are doing wrong things. He speaks His promises to our hearts. He talks to us through our consciences. He leads us through good and bad situations. It is important to know the promises of God.

...But they who wait for the Lord shall renew their strength; they shall mount up with wings like eagles; they shall run and not be weary; they shall walk and not faint (Isaiah 40:31).

Many of God's promises are given to let us know that He will help us. He will strengthen us. He will give us peace. He loves us, and even though we live in a sinful world, we do not fear.

Our only responsibilities to receive God promises are to love Him, confess our sins, and follow Christ. God promises eternal life through Christ's death on the cross in our place. We don't have to die on a cross to receive it, even though we deserve to.

Living life knowing the promises of God and that He never fails to keep them gives us peace and confidence. It is more than we could ever imagine and continues through good times and bad. We can rejoice when others can't. We can stand when others fall.

> **"And now I am about to go the way of all the earth, and you know in your hearts and souls, all of you, that not one word has failed of all the good things that the Lord your God promised concerning you. All have come to pass for you; not one of them has failed" (Joshua 23:14).**

It is difficult to live as a follower of Christ in a sinful world, but God is working out His plan to bring us all back into relationship with Him. Evil will not win. God has promised, and it will be so.

> **For the wages of sin is death, but the free gift of God is eternal life in Christ Jesus our Lord (Romans 6:23).**

> *Prayer:* **God, we know that you are with us always, when times are good and through times when life is stressful and full of trouble. You promise us we can have peace as we trust that you are in control of everything, and we know you keep your promises. Help us hold your promises in our hearts and know your peace. Amen.**

Blessed Comfort

> **Blessed are those who mourn, for they shall be comforted (Matthew 5:4).**

Loss hurts. It doesn't matter if it is the loss of a loved one, a pet, a job, a friend, or an ability; it hurts. Some losses hurt more than others. Some hurts last longer. We have all suffered the loss of someone or something; but hopefully, we have never lost God.

We should say God has never lost us. He never leaves. He never gives up on us. He never forgets about us or turns away. If it weren't for God, how could we get through the losses in our lives? The Holy Spirit gives us peace to help us through these losses, and we are who we are in part because of these losses.

> **Blessed be the God and Father of our Lord Jesus Christ, the Father of mercies and God of all comfort, who comforts us in all our affliction, so that we may be able to comfort those who are in any affliction, with the comfort with which we ourselves are comforted by God (2 Corinthians 1:3-4).**

Even God has suffered loss. He lost His son for a time when Christ went to retrieve the keys to death, hell, and the grave. The children of Israel turned away from Him. The world today doesn't even believe He exists. How much that must hurt our Father.

How many people have turned from their creator to worship other things? And what about us, the Christians? Do we worship Him for who He is, or for what He can give us?

Jesus suffered loss. He lost Judas, one of His beloved apostles. He lost when all His followers scattered after His arrest. He lost when the people, who had previously worshiped Him, called for His crucifixion, and He lost His life for us.

> **He will wipe away every tear from their eyes, and death shall be no more, neither shall there be mourning, nor crying, nor pain anymore, for the former things have passed away (Revelation 21:4).**

When we suffer loss, we grieve. We may cry and blame ourselves or blame God. But we have peace when we remember that even though this world is under the influence of the evil one, God will make good come out of everything that happens for those who believe in Him.

> **And we know that in all things God works for the good of those who love him, who have been called according to his purpose (Romans 8:28).**

When we suffer a loss, we know that our Lord is near. His Holy Spirit is our comforter. The closer we draw to Him, the easier our grief will be to bear. We may not understand why things happen when they do, but we know that our God loves us. If we look back on our lives, we can see that He has always been there and gotten us through the pain. He will get us through again.

> **The Lord is near to the brokenhearted and saves the crushed in spirit (Psalm 24:18).**

We must call on God in our time of need and breathe in His peace and comfort. Trust grows each time we look to God for peace in times of loss. Though this is not easy to do, we are certain that He is working in our lives.

> **Peace I leave with you; my peace I give to you. Not as the world gives do I give to you. Let not your hearts be troubled, neither let them be afraid (John 14:27).**

Reading God's word will remind us who made the world and everything in it, who has suffered the greatest loss, and whom it is that is standing with us through it all.

> **He heals the brokenhearted and binds up their wounds (Psalm 147:3).**

> *Prayer:* **Lord, when our hearts break, let us remember your heart and your love. When loss comes to our lives, give us your comfort and your peace. When loss comes to others, help us to show them the way to you and to comfort them with the comfort you have given us. Amen.**

We Are Frustrated Lord

You keep [us] in perfect peace whose mind is stayed on you, because [we] trust in you (Isaiah 26:3 *Jenni's paraphrase*).

Some days, it seems that one thing after another goes wrong. Maybe we oversleep, then we drop our coffee, the phone rings when we are in the shower, and it is a telemarketer, then the dog throws up, our boss doesn't listen to us—again—and we are late to an appointment. Why do these things happen? The laws of nature at work in a crazy world can make us crazy too, but we can have peace through all of it, or we can get frustrated.

Trust in the Lord with all your heart, and do not lean on your own understanding. In all your ways acknowledge him, and he will make straight your paths (Proverbs 3:5,6).

Frustration can last for a few minutes or a few weeks. It is not a straight path, and it is a tool used by the powers of darkness, but it is really up to us how long we allow it to last. Frustration with life is not pleasant. It makes us grit our teeth and clench our fists, and it darkens our minds and thoughts.

Frustration, if allowed to linger or come upon us often, is the opposite of trusting in the Lord. It gives an opportunity to the devil to move in and create havoc in our lives. We shouldn't beat ourselves up for a little frustration now and then, but if we are quick to become frustrated and slow to let it go, it can lead to anger and other issues.

Of course, if we allow the frustration to continue, things usually get worse. If we can view life with a peaceful heart and a calm mind, frustration will only last a second before we remember that God is in control. Peace from the Holy Spirit can melt that frustration away and give us a new perspective on the events around us.

Be not quick in your spirit to become angry, for anger lodges in the bosom of fools (Ecclesiastes 7:9).

Our brains are capable of producing thousands of thoughts per day. Most of these thoughts are repeated daily and reflect our mindset or beliefs. So, if our thoughts are tinged with frustration, negativity, and anger, that will be what our focus is on instead of the things of the Lord.

> **Good sense makes [us] slow to anger, and it is [our] glory to overlook an offense (Proverbs 19:11 *Jenni's paraphrase*).**

We don't want frustration to overtake us, make us cry, take our focus from good, positive things, and turn us to anger. We want to have good sense. We know we don't need to be frustrated. We are children of the living God, but we are also human. The important thing is not to let the frustration persist or take control of our emotions.

God cares about even the smallest frustrations. He will never leave us alone to deal with any of it. The 'small stuff' that sometimes gets to us is important to our heavenly father, which means we don't have to worry about it.

> **Fear not, for I am with you; be not dismayed, for I am your God; I will strengthen you, I will help you, I will uphold you with my righteous right hand (Isaiah 41:10).**

Our prayer on those days when everything goes wrong, and we get frustrated, is that God will have us pause and help us to calm down and to slow down.

Life is difficult, and life as a Christian is sometimes a struggle, too. Thankfully, unlike those who don't know God, we have a comforter who is always with us. God is the perfect friend. He is always there, always listening, always helping, and is not demanding.

Fight frustration with prayer. Be assured that God loves us, and when crazy things happen, try to smile through it all.

> *Prayer:* **Lord, life gets crazy sometimes, and frustration can get the better of us. Help us to laugh in the face of this craziness. Let others see the peace you give to us and the calm way we respond so that they will see what a great God we have in all that we do and say. Amen.**

Patience:
The fourth fruit of the Holy Spirit

> **But the fruit of the Spirit is love, joy, peace, patience, kindness, goodness, faithfulness, gentleness, and self-control. Against such things there is no Law. And those who belong to Christ Jesus have crucified the flesh with its passions and desires. If we live by the Spirit, let us also keep in step with the Spirit (Galatians 5:22-25).**

Hupomoné: a remaining behind, a patient enduring

Short Definition: endurance, steadfastness

Definition: endurance, steadfastness, patiently waiting for.

Patience implies waiting or enduring suffering. It determines our will. We choose to wait patiently. God is patient with us, meaning that He endures uncomplainingly. Patience is a Christian virtue.

> **May the God who gives endurance (patience) and encouragement give you the same attitude of mind toward each other that Christ Jesus had (Romans 15:5).**

God is patient with us, and He grants us patience with each other. It is in our reliance on Him, trusting and following Christ's example, that we can patiently wait on God. We have a steadfast hope as we wait for God and patiently wait on each other.

The God of Patience

Or do you presume on the riches of his kindness and forbearance and patience, not knowing that God's kindness is meant to lead you to repentance? (Romans 2:4).

Grace, love, kindness, forbearance, and patience are some of God's characteristics. They are available to us through Him and are to be used to the benefit of others. He is so patient with our shortcomings and desires that we are patient with each other, so all may come to know Him.

Someday, you will see someone in our church, maybe a young person or even a long-time Christian, do something we know is a sin. Maybe they really hurt you or someone else, got a DUI, or had an affair.

Let's say that a young single Christian high school girl from our church gets pregnant. Do we have a baby shower as we would for a married woman? To some, these are tough questions, but hopefully, to us, the answers are clear. Christ's kindness, forbearance, and patience will lead us to repentance. He loves everyone the same and so should we.

Some Christians feel that we can righteously turn away from such people. They know that the person has sinned, so they feel justified in ignoring, answering back, or reprimanding the sinner and letting them know that God is not happy with what they did. They call their behavior *righteous indignation.*

Often, we treat others the same way they are treating us. We may react with anger, disappointment, or disgust and feel perfectly justified in doing so. Christ's reaction would have been love and patience.

If we have a choice to be angry with someone and point out the error of their ways, or to be gracious and kind, and we don't know what choice to make, we will never go wrong if we err on the side of grace and patience as we follow Christ's example.

What this means is that yes, you would have a baby shower. God is patient with everyone the same as He is patient with us, no matter who they are or what they have done. We need to do the same. We need to show the world God's love and patience.

It is never our right to judge or believe it is up to us to teach them a lesson. Our job is to give grace and mercy as God gives grace and mercy to all.

> **Love is patient and kind; love does not envy or boast; it is not arrogant (1 Corinthians 13:4).**

If we ever question how to react or act when we hear about something someone has done, err on the side of grace and patience. We will never be wrong in God's eyes if we love.

Christ did not use harsh words towards sinners. He ate with them and spent time with them. He told the disciples that He did not come to save the righteous, but to the save the sinners. If we are examples of Christ to the world, we must have the same attitude as Christ.

> **Whoever is slow to anger has great understanding, but he who has a hasty temper exalts folly (Proverbs 14:29).**

Having the patience of God means that when a car pulls out in front of us or cuts us off, we give them the benefit of the doubt. We don't decide that they are terrible drivers and get angry and try to get ahead of them. When the waitress at the restaurant is in a terrible mood, we pray for her or give her a smile to brighten her day.

When a Christian brother or sister makes a bad choice, we pray for them or take them to lunch, and when a young person follows peer pressure into sin, we love them anyway.

Our patience can have a positive effect on those around us. This attitude will show them the love of Christ and help to lead them to the one who gave His life.

Christians who become judgmental, being impatient with those who fail, and believing that they are always right, are committing the sin of self-righteousness. Being patient requires a humble heart to succeed.

> **And from his fullness we have all received, grace upon grace (John 1:1).**

> ***Prayer*: Lord, let us remember how blessed we are and how much you love us even when we fail. You are so pa-**

tient in teaching us your ways. Let us be patient with others. We thank you, our father. Help us not to ask ourselves whether we should give grace to those around us, but to ask ourselves how much grace we can give. Amen.

Bigotry and Discrimination

There is neither Jew nor Greek, there is neither slave nor free, there is no male and female, for you are all one in Christ Jesus (Gal. 3:28).

In Bible times, many groups hated each other, i.e., Jews, Gentiles, Samaritans, and Greeks. Their bigotry or discrimination was mostly based on their religious beliefs or lack of belief in any deity.

God evidently loved diversity since He created people with different colors, heights, eyes, etc. He created different animals and many different plants. Humans, however, found reasons to hate each other because of their differences.

Whole communities were full of one belief group or other. Samaritans didn't like Jews passing through their area. It is not mentioned whether any of these bigotries were based on the color of skin, but they seemed to have plenty of other reasons for disliking each other. There have been wars because of bigotry, and there still are.

Today we also have issues with discrimination, and it is getting worse, which is what the Bible predicted would happen. Many Christians are not helping the situation. Some are adding to the fear, violence, and bigotry. Christians involving themselves with hate groups are causing division. Christians are picketing, fighting, yelling, and arguing with each other and with nonbelievers. How can we show Christ's love to all if we are behaving the same way that non-Christians are behaving?

As Christians, we know where we stand. We stand on the cross of Christ. Christians are all one body and the family of God, no matter their race or sex. Christ taught us to love everyone, Christian or not. We are told to hate the sin and love the sinner.

While Jesus was having dinner at Levi's house, many tax collectors and sinners were eating with him and his disciples, for there were many who followed him. When the teachers of the law who were Pharisees saw him eating with the sinners and tax collectors, they asked his disciples: "Why does he eat with tax collectors and sinners?" (Mark 2:15,16).

Jesus did not and does not discriminate. He wants everyone to know Him, love Him, and to follow Him. He loves every person just as they are and has patience with them while He works in their lives to bring them into His kingdom. He will forgive their sins when they come to Him. If we are to follow His example, then it is our responsibility to do the same.

Each of Christ's disciples came from different backgrounds, and He used each of them to spread the gospel after His death and resurrection. The religious people of the day wanted to know why He was associating with sinners and He told them.

> **"I have not come to call the righteous but sinners to repentance" (Luke 5:32).**

There are many sins that the world deems acceptable in our society, and we cannot pretend as if there is nothing wrong, but we must still love the person who is living in sin. We know that all sins are unacceptable to God, and therefore, to us, but we can't confuse the sin with the person who is sinning. The powers of darkness that are ruling this world blind them. We need to show them the love and patience of God and bring them out of their sin.

Doing something with or for a non-Christian or someone whose views differ from our own, does not mean that we agree with them. Though we don't want evil to influence us or spend a lot of time with the evil in the world, we can never go wrong when loving those around us as Christ did. How much better for us, when we associate with people who are sinning, to be patient and show the love of Christ by our actions and our lifestyles? Christ came to save the lost, and we want to help, not get in the way.

We must never turn away from someone in need, no matter what they believe, or anyone who does not know the Lord and needs salvation. We can be their friends and show them God's love without getting into arguments or causing hurt. We must be as patient as God is, even with those who are discriminating against us.

> **There is only one lawgiver and judge, he who is able to save and to destroy. But who are you to judge your neighbor (James 4:12).**

God is always going before us and knocking at the door of sinners' hearts. He is patiently revealing the truth to them even when they refuse to hear His voice. It is not for us to judge when we know that God is the only lawgiver and judge.

God will save, and He asks us to work at showing and telling the world the good news of Jesus Christ. We all sin and need forgiveness. We cannot cast the first stone at anyone. Discriminating is a sin for the Christian.

> **For if we go on sinning deliberately after receiving the knowledge of the truth, there no longer remains a sacrifice for sins (Hebrews 10:26).**

No one is perfect except Jesus Christ. If we, who are sinful, become judgmental about people who are committing various sins, we start creating a hierarchy of sins where one is worse than another. Sin is sin, and if we think that our sins aren't that important, then we are in error. Self-righteousness can also be a sin.

The only difference between Christians and those who don't know Christ yet is that we bring our sins to God and He forgives us if we make every effort to refrain from sinning again. We know that when we ask God to forgive our sins, He will do so.

For us to judge when He tells us not to, and for us to hate those whom He loves is more than an insult to God. It is discrimination and bigotry.

God hates sin, but He loved us while we were still sinners and He loves those who are still sinning. Let us love sinners the way He loved us and show them that eternal life with God can only be had through the blood of Jesus.

> **For I know that nothing good dwells in me, that is, in my flesh. For I have the desire to do what is right, but not the ability to carry it out (Romans 7:28).**

> *Prayer:* **God, help us live upright lives according to your word. Help us be loving and patient with all people, hating sin, but acting with kindness to sinners so that they will know that you love them too. God, keep us under the**

blood of our Lord, Jesus, continually seeking forgiveness of our sins and sincerely striving to do what is right in your sight. As sin surrounds us that the world says is acceptable, let us stay focused on the truth of your word. Help us to show this truth and your love to this world by our actions and our words. Amen.

Waiting on the Lord

The Lord is good to those who wait for him, to the soul who seeks him (Lamentations 3:25).

Oh, how we hate to wait. We are not a patient people. Waiting in line, waiting to hear news, waiting to move into a new house, waiting for a flight, waiting for vacation, waiting for traffic, waiting, waiting! But God tells us that He is good to those who wait for Him and seek Him. In that instance, waiting is a good thing.

Waiting on the Lord is important, but we have lost the ability to wait patiently. We are a society of instant gratification. If the microwave takes 5 minutes to cook our dinner, we think that is too long. When we apply for a job, we want to know if we got it right then. When did we get in such a hurry to have and to do everything?

In earlier generations, everything took longer. It took longer to get anywhere and longer to cook. They waited on their crops for seasons, months, and years without complaint. Now when we are forced to wait, we don't do it well. So how can we learn to wait on God when waiting seems to have become such a negative thing?

The original Greek for 'wait' translates as 'waiting in hope with eager expectation.' Waiting on God is trusting that He will carry out what needs doing, and we do not have to worry about it. The good news is that we can wait on God's move even while we are waiting in line or in traffic. God's plans will come to pass. Waiting takes patience.

But they who wait for the Lord shall renew their strength; they shall mount up with wings like eagles; they shall run and not be weary; they shall walk and not faint (Isaiah 40:31).

Waiting with patience will strengthen us. When we try to jump in and take over without waiting, things can go terribly wrong, but we tend to act instead of waiting. We may feel that God wants something accomplished, so we wait a little while, and then we roll up our sleeves and go about trying to make it happen. It usually fails because of our impatience in waiting on God's timing.

When God is leading us, we must take steps along the way, but forcing things to happen faster than God's timing will not make it come to pass any sooner or any better. God's timing is perfect. We may not always understand why, but we need to wait on the Lord.

> **Trust in the Lord with all your heart, and do not lean on your own understanding. In all your ways acknowledge him, and he will make straight your paths (Proverbs 3:5-6).**

Waiting is a positive experience. The Holy Spirit will give us patience if we ask for it. When we are in line for something, in a hurry, frustrated over the time that everything is taking, and we are waiting impatiently, we can ask God for His Holy Spirit to give us the patience that we need. We can ask for patience to wait at that moment, and He will give it to us.

Sometimes people say, "don't pray for patience or God will put you through a trial." This is not true. God doesn't work that way. Though He may use situations to teach us, He is not going to cause something to make us wait so that we can learn patience. It is a fruit of the Spirit and is given freely to those who ask.

> ***Prayer:*** **Lord, you know patience is not easy for us. We seem to always be in a hurry. Help us to wait for your guidance, your patience, your leading in our daily lives. More than anything, help us to wait on you, being still and letting you be our Father. Amen.**

Planning Your Future

Many are the plans in the mind of a man, but it is the purpose of the Lord that will stand (Proverbs 19:21).

We like to plan, and many are the plans in the mind of man. How well God knows us. We like to know what is going to happen, and we like to have things to look forward to, but when we plan something and rush to do it, sometimes it doesn't work out.

Knowing when or if we should plan is something we question. Planning for something that is not in God's plan will usually fail, so Christians sometimes feel that we shouldn't plan at all. "God's running the show" is something we hear, and yes, it is true (or at least God should be running the show), but He won't be if we don't let Him. Should we plan? Should we not plan?

Come now, you who say, "Today or tomorrow we will go into such and such a town and spend a year there and trade and make a profit"— yet you do not know what tomorrow will bring. What is your life? For you are a mist that appears for a little time and then vanishes. Instead you ought to say, "If the Lord wills, we will live and do this or that" (James 4:13-15).

We could plan something and tell ourselves and others "If God wills, I will do such." This is biblical if we are allowing God to have control of our lives, being patient and waiting for His leading. We shouldn't fool ourselves, though, or try to fool God. Is it our intention to do whatever we have planned, whether God wills it or not?

We can ask God for knowledge and wisdom while we plan. He will give it to us. Our conscience and our gut feelings about our plans are often God's way of telling us yes or no. Still, we are unsure whether planning is a good idea.

If any of you lacks wisdom, let him ask God, who gives generously to all without reproach, and it will be given him (James 1:5).

We have free will. We can make things happen that aren't in our best interest. God will allow us to make these mistakes. That is why planning is difficult, but with a little common sense and a lot of prayer, we will know what we can plan and what we should not.

God wants us to plan. He doesn't want us to just flop around, waiting for some miraculous sign from Him. The apostles made plans for their journeys, and yet, waited on God for the right times.

It is perfectly okay for us to make plans, to hope that certain things will happen, to have goals. God just wants in on the planning. What is important is communication with God, waiting on Him, and making sure our plans agree with His word.

The heart of man plans his way, but the Lord establishes his steps (Proverbs 16:9).

If, in our planning, we make sure that our communication with God is open and honest and we delve deep into our hearts to discern what is driving the plan, whether it is selfish or not, we are assured that the Lord will establish our steps.

It is not wrong to say, "I hope when I retire, I can do this or that" or "when I graduate, I plan to become this or that," as long as we commit our ways to the Lord and allow Him to open and close doors without stepping in to force them.

What we can't plan is the duration of certain plans of the Lord. Often God takes more time than usual to complete His plans. We can't plan who or when someone will accept the Lord, but we can plan how we will talk to them about Him. We can be patient, let God establish our steps, and wait for His leading in all things.

Commit your work to the Lord, and your plans will be established (Proverbs 16:3).

***Prayer*: Lord, remind us that you are with us every step of the way. Planning with you makes the journey more joyous and our plans more fruitful. Help us be patient as we allow your leading in our lives and allow you to establish our steps. Let us know when to plan and when not to plan. We trust in you. Amen.**

Entitlement

For even when we were with you, we would give you this command: If anyone is not willing to work, let him not eat (2 Thessalonians 3:10).

As Christians, we are entitled to a lot. God's promises are for us, and we are entitled to what He has promised. There are thousands of promises from God in the Bible, and He keeps every one of them.

Most importantly, we are entitled to eternal life if we ask Christ to forgive our sins and we follow Him. We are entitled to the fruit of His Holy Spirit, no matter what is going on in our lives.

We are entitled to God's love, guidance, and help at all times when we give Him our hearts and make Him the center of our existence.

What we are not entitled to, however, is everything we ever ask for. We are not entitled to react with anger when we are not chosen for the church board, or someone sits in our special seat. We are not entitled to inclusion in the pastor's inner circle or to have God as our fairy godmother granting all our wishes.

There are people in this world who are gracious and generous, who say things like "I have enough, please give this to others." There are also those with an attitude of entitlement who are greedy and say things like "Where is mine? What's in it for me?" and "I deserve better." As Christians, we are to think of others before ourselves.

Do nothing from selfish ambition or conceit, but in humility count others more significant than yourselves (Philippians 2:3).

When did we start feeling that we are entitled to be fed, to be happy, to have a TV, a car, a cell phone? Are we entitled to these things, which means they are given to us? Or are we entitled to work for them and save for them?

We hear, "We deserve to be happy." Do we? Who says? Many of us were raised by parents who went through the depression. We learned to work and create our own happiness. Is happiness a right?

Joy is one of the fruits of the spirit, so even when things aren't going as the world thinks they should, we can have an attitude of rejoicing.

But we are not promised happiness as the world views happiness. Joy comes from patiently waiting on the Lord for our needs to be met, not getting angry because we haven't received the things to which we feel entitled.

> **For everyone who exalts himself will be humbled, and he who humbles himself will be exalted (Luke 14:11).**

It is difficult to live in the world today seeing what is on TV and all the supposed happiness that comes from worldly pleasures. It is hard not to feel entitled when some, who don't work as hard, have more than we do or are seemingly much happier. We can become jealous when others are given places of honor that we feel we deserve.

We need to remember TV is fake, and often what we see in others is a façade. It is better that Christians be patient and humble and show what we are truly entitled to—that is, God's great promises and love. We should not view ourselves with the world's standards. True happiness comes only from knowing God and yielding patiently to His plan.

Christians are entitled to all of God's promises in God's time, and we are more blessed than anyone else because of it. We don't choose worldly entitlement.

> ***Prayer:* Dear God, help us to remember that the happiness of this world is fleeting, and the things of this world will not give us your joy. Help us remember that we are not entitled to the things of the world, nor should we want them. Take all selfishness out of us, and may we always give the highest places of honor to others. Amen.**

Hearing the Voice of God

> **When the Spirit of truth comes, he will guide you into all the truth, for he will not speak on his own authority, but whatever he hears he will speak, and he will declare to you the things that are to come (John 16:13).**

The ways God speaks to us vary, and there are many. Hearing Him is sometimes a challenge. To hear God, we must have a close personal relationship with Him. It requires regular conversation without us doing all the talking. We must patiently wait for God to speak, and we must listen for the spirit of truth.

If we are only approaching God with our needs and wants, and if we are never still or listening for His voice, we will miss it. Though God can speak to us through very clear and miraculous ways, that is generally not how we hear from Him.

God uses our mind, who some call our spirit (as in body, soul, and spirit). Whatever we call it, the more communication time we have with Him, the more His voice will be in our minds. Since He is always with us, we should always be in conversation and ready to hear what He has to say.

> **My sheep hear my voice, and I know them, and they follow me (John 10:27).**

When God does not talk back immediately or what we hear is not what we wanted, we may become frustrated and disregard it as not coming from Him. Frustration means we are not patiently waiting to hear from Him. He is patient with us, though, and will often repeat Himself so that we don't miss His message. There are no tricks to hearing from God. He is our Father, He hears us when we talk to Him, and He talks back.

We all hear from God, although many aren't aware that He is speaking. Sometimes He speaks through our conscience, or through a song, or through a message at church. Sometimes He speaks through others to confirm what we have already heard but are unsure of.

Sometimes He speaks to us when we can't sleep, suggesting people who need prayer or revealing a message that He would like us to take to them. Prayer is not the only way He speaks to us.

> **And your ears shall hear a word behind you, saying, "This is the way, walk in it," when you turn to the right or when you turn to the left (Isaiah 30:21).**

Reading His word and communicating with Him about every aspect of our lives will make it easier to recognize His voice over others. God's voice will never contradict His word. That is key. Other voices are worldly, unkind, contradictory, angry, or manipulative. Other voices will not speak kindly of God.

God is not sneaky. God is love. If the voice we hear is not filled with love, it is not God. In reading or listening to God's word, we will know what the mind of God is. Then, when He speaks, we will know it is Him if it aligns with His word. We need to patiently wait for God to speak.

We often talk about asking God for wisdom and knowledge and yet have no idea how to recognize when they are given to us. We are confident that God is giving us what He promised, but it is our responsibility to discern His voice above the rest.

> **So faith comes from hearing, and hearing through the word of Christ (Romans 10:17).**

Let us consider Romans 10:17, which is a verse we often struggle with. Here is an explanation: our faith is stronger, and our relationship with the Father becomes greater when we hear from Him. So, faith comes from hearing from God.

We hear from Him because we read His word and follow it. So, hearing comes from reading the word. The more we read, the more we hear, and the greater our faith becomes.

This life cycle brings both knowledge and wisdom, helping us to patiently wait to grow in grace until we can recognize the voice of God.

The accuser of this world, the devil, will try to speak, but God will overpower that voice. Listen only to the goodness of God. His voice is only good. When good thoughts come repeatedly, we need to pray about them, and God will confirm them in our hearts. We should not immediately rush to act on what we hear but use wisdom and prayer to make sure it is from God.

If He speaks a word for us to give to someone else that is encouraging and uplifting, we cannot be afraid to pass it on. An encouraging word will not do harm, even if it is just from us, if we do not share it with pride as if we were special because we think we heard from God.

We should take care of becoming prideful because we hear His voice. Hearing from God is not our focus. Our focus is a stronger relationship with Him. We will hear from God in His time; we must be patient. He does not speak in our time. As we become more spiritually mature, we will hear Him more clearly.

> *Prayer:* **Father, thank you for speaking to us clearly through our minds, through others, and through your word. Help us to patiently wait on you while we listen and learn, read and follow, and grow spiritually into the people you want us to be. Use us to encourage others. Cleanse us from our pride and other sins. We wait patiently to hear from you. Amen.**

Do We Really Believe in God?

And he said to them, "Why are you troubled, and why do doubts arise in your hearts?" (Luke 24:38).

Strange emotions come when doubts creep into our minds about God. We can feel confused and feel that we have betrayed God. We should understand that doubting God does not make us unbelievers. Doubt is not the complete absence of faith and is temporary.

If we are having doubts about God's existence on a regular basis, we should seek counsel with our pastor or a Christian we respect. These thoughts are spiritually detrimental. We should repent when these thoughts come up, and we can chase them out by prayer and rebuking the devil. If we dwell on our doubts, we give them power, allowing them to draw us away from God.

Impatience in life, when we take control and move God out of the center, is a momentary lack of faith, but we all do it. That lack of faith is more about "will God handle this?" not "Does God exist?" These are normal moments in every Christian's life. Patience is sometimes a troublesome battle.

Questioning God's existence causes problems with our faith. The world tells us that He isn't real, that He is a myth, or even worse, one of many ways to heaven. We hear it so often, we may start to believe the world's lies. The world is under the control of the powers of darkness, and we are in a battle for our minds and hearts.

Be sober-minded; be watchful. Your adversary the devil prowls around like a roaring lion, seeking someone to devour (1 Peter 5:8).

The lie that makes us question the reality of God comes from the accuser, the devil. Evil is everywhere and is more prevalent today than before. We can't let evil cause us to doubt the great love and care that God has blessed us with. We need to have patience with ourselves as He is patient with us and we grow closer to Him.

When someone comes along with a theory that makes us question our belief in God and wonder if He really loves us, answers our prayers, and guides our lives, we should look back and remember the times that He has. He has worked out situations for each of us that seemed impossible, and we know that He is real. Our belief is strong and true. God will bring them to our remembrance.

And have mercy on those who doubt (Jude 1:22).

God understands our struggles. We are human, we have failings, and our minds often wander to dangerous places. Continual communication with Him keeps our minds focused on the truth of His existence and thankful for His patience with us as we constantly grow stronger in Him.

Avoid disputes about Christianity with nonbelievers. Read God's word and pray. Then, take a walk outside. Paul says in Romans that what we see in this world will tell us that God exists just by being there. What God has created is majestic and amazing. We have no excuse for doubt.

For what can be known about God is plain to them, because God has shown it to them. For his invisible attributes, namely, his eternal power and divine nature, have been clearly perceived, ever since the creation of the world, in the things that have been made. So they are without excuse (Romans 1:19-20).

God is king of the world. Seeing His creation, feeling His power, hearing His voice, and reading His word will keep our minds on the blessings we have been given and keep us watching for the wonders He works in our lives.

But these are written so that you may believe that Jesus is the Christ, the Son of God, and that by believing you may have life in his name (John 20:31).

Prayer: **Jesus, your death on the cross saved us, and yet sometimes we doubt the very existence of God. Forgive us for these times and help us to stay focused on you and your love. Thank you for your patience with us as we struggle through this world that is making our lives more difficult. Help us trust you more. Amen.**

A New Day

Because of the tender mercy of our God, whereby the sunrise shall visit us from on high to give light to those who sit in darkness and in the shadow of death, to guide our feet into the way of peace (Luke 1:78-79).

Every day is a new day. Every morning we have new mercies from the Lord. God will forgive our sins every time we ask Him, and He will never stop loving us and guiding us. He is always faithful and keeps His promises.

Life may feel like it kicks us when we are down, but tomorrow, everything can change in an instant. We must wait patiently for God's timing. He is always working for our good. We can not give up.

God's faithfulness never ends, though our patience is often weak and our faith in Him wavers. Each new day, we should be determined to hold on to His faithfulness. Even when everything seems to be falling apart, we can know that God is faithful even when we are not.

Our responsibility is to avoid temptations, to refrain from what we know is sin, to be faithful to God's word, and to be patient. We often fail, but God tells us that He is still with us. He will not fail us.

We want things to be in our timing, but God's timing is perfect, and His way is best. We may need to wait for a new day. Our greatest responsibility is to not give up on God and to not give up on life.

When we are struggling in life, we believe things will never change. When we are sick, we feel that we will be sick forever. When we see what others have, we may think we will never have a life like them. But when we are faithful and patient, things can change in a moment. Our past is not our future. Each day brings new mercies.

For I know the plans I have for you, declares the Lord, plans for welfare and not for evil, to give you a future and a hope. Then you will call upon me and come and pray to me, and I will hear you (Jeremiah 29:11-12).

God will provide what we need when we need it. It may not be what we want or when we want it. He is not working to make us temporarily happy, but to give us eternal joy. He wants our relationship with Him to be stronger so that we not only know Him, but we have the constant assurance that He will take care of us.

Through belief in Jesus Christ, His death on the cross for our sins, and His resurrection, we will be returned to right relationship with God. Still, we must live in this evil world. He understands our struggles. He will provide new mercies every day. We can sleep, trusting that new things will happen tomorrow.

> **The steadfast love of the Lord never ceases; his mercies never come to an end; they are new every morning; great is your faithfulness (Lamentations 3:22-23).**

Each day when we rise, if we focus on the simple message of salvation and how much God loves us, our spirits will be lifted. It is important to thank God each day for His faithfulness and the assurance of His presence, knowing that we do not need to fear anything.

When we need encouragement or comfort, God will provide them. He will give us the strength to get through trials. We are the strong ones. We have a faithful God.

> **But they who wait for the Lord shall renew their strength; they shall mount up with wings like eagles; they shall run and not be weary; they shall walk and not faint (Isaiah 40:31).**

God will keep us safe from the evil one. When it seems that all is lost and so bad that we may want to leave this world, we must remember His promises and that each new day, each new year brings more mercy and grace from God. Tomorrow is a new day.

Be faithful in all things for the Lord, and look toward the light that will chase away the darkness from our lives. Who knows what tomorrow holds? God does.

> ***Prayer*: Lord, lift our spirits when we are down and strengthen our faith when it is weak. Each day let us come to you and know your love and faithfulness. We trust that you are working out good plans for our lives. Help us to wait on you. We know your timing is perfect, and we wait expectantly and thankfully for your blessings. Amen.**

Kindness:
The fifth fruit of the Holy Spirit

> **But the fruit of the Spirit is love, joy, peace, patience, kindness, goodness, faithfulness, gentleness, and self-control. Against such things there is no Law. And those who belong to Christ Jesus have crucified the flesh with its passions and desires. If we live by the Spirit, let us also keep in step with the Spirit (Galatians 5:22-25).**

The word 'kindness' is translated as 'charis' more frequently than any other translation. Charis **is defined as (a) grace, as a gift or blessing brought to man by Jesus Christ, (b) favor, (c) gratitude, thanks, (d) a favor, kindness**.

The biblical use of the word kindness means so much more than what we consider to be kindness today. **Biblestudytool.com** says that kindness is an attribute of God and a quality desirable but not consistently found in humans.

Kindness is the grace given to us by God, a blessing brought by Jesus. It is also a fruit of the Holy Spirit that we can seek so that we are kind to others. God has told us to be kind.

> **Note then the kindness and the severity of God: severity toward those who have fallen, but God's kindness to you, provided you continue in his kindness. Otherwise you too will be cut off (Romans 11:22).**

The God of Kindness

A man who is kind benefits himself, but a cruel man hurts himself (Proverbs 11:17).

There are two ways the Christian experiences kindness. We feel God's kindness to us, and we show kindness to others.

God's kindness is easy to understand. It is in His love towards us and draws us ever closer to Him. He loves us and gave His only son to die in our place.

God's kindness is also seen in His help for us at times of affliction and need. His kindness is in everything He does or doesn't do and is an example to us so that we will repent of our sins and be kind to others.

There is so much cruelty in the world today. We see it on the news every night. People are being hateful to each other, to groups with differing beliefs, to their families, and to themselves. There is cruelty to children and animals, and yet, if we ask people if they consider themselves as kind, most would probably say yes.

Today's society believes that unkindness is acceptable when it suits us and kindness when it is convenient. We are a self-serving, self-centered people. Sometimes we even behave kindly on the outside when inside we are thinking hateful thoughts.

Little children, let us not love in word or talk but in deed and in truth (1 John 3:18).

Kindness is not easy when your co-worker takes credit for your work or the person that bumped into you doesn't even say 'excuse me.' In almost every situation today, there is a chance that someone will be unkind, and it is difficult, even for Christians, to react with kind thoughts and deeds.

Our thoughts may immediately jump to a negative response, which is sometimes followed by an unkind action. But we serve the God of kindness, who is constantly teaching us through our experiences to respond with kindness in every situation.

Christians are called to a higher standard than the world. We are unselfish, Christ-centered people. We think kind thoughts as well as being kind in our actions.

At times, it may seem like we are allowing the world to take advantage of us, but look at Christ's example of kindness. His love and understanding of the people and why they did what they did was so great that He could be kind even when He was in great pain while dying on the cross.

We don't know what each unkind person is going through, why they act as they do, or what evil holds them. They are God's children. He loves them and wants to bring them into a right relationship with Him. Our kind reaction to their unkindness could be a turning point.

On our own, we cannot be kind. We can imagine being kind. We can fake it, but we cannot bring true kindness into being without God's help. The Holy Spirit is the helper that will strengthen us and help us to bring forth the fruit of kindness.

Having received the Holy Spirit when we accepted Christ into our hearts, we have access to the fruit of kindness, and if we seek it diligently and practice daily, it will become a natural part of our being. Having Christ as the center of all is the key to being kind to those around us.

> **Be kind to one another, tenderhearted, forgiving one another, as God in Christ forgave you (Eph. 4:32).**

> **Do not repay evil for evil or reviling for reviling, but on the contrary, bless, for to this you were called, that you may obtain a blessing (1 Peter 3:9).**

God's kindness manifests itself, not just in giving, but in goodwill, tolerance, and understanding of other's actions and beliefs. Sympathy and grace are part of kindness, not just when we agree, but especially when we do not. The truth about kindness is that it is not easy, but thankfully we serve the God of kindness who will help us.

What does the God of kindness ask of us? He has made it very clear in Micah.

> **He has told you, O man, what is good; and what does the Lord require of you but to do justice, and to love kindness, and to walk humbly with your God (Micah 6:8).**

***Prayer:* Lord, you have made it clear that we are to love kindness. You know that this is difficult for us, but with your help, we can understand its importance in this world. Thank you for giving us your Holy Spirit to help us react and act with kindness to everyone we meet and to our friends and family. Amen.**

Understanding Anger

Be not quick in your spirit to become angry, for anger lodges in the bosom of fools (Ecclesiastes 7:9).

Anger is common, and is the opposite of kindness. But what is anger, really? When we analyze our anger, we will discover that we may not be angry at all. As an emotion, anger is attributed to many reactions that are not really produced by anger. It is a catch-all word for a variety of emotions that manifest themselves in similar ways.

We need to understand what the word *anger* means when used in the Bible.

Biblestudytools.com defines anger as a strong emotional reaction of displeasure, often leading to plans for revenge or punishment. There are many words for anger in Hebrew; in Greek, orge [o jrghv] and thumos [qumov] are used more or less interchangeably.

We can agree that a strong emotional reaction of displeasure is often what we feel when we are angry. However, we often use the word *anger* when we are frustrated, embarrassed, scared, sad, insecure, stressed out, intimidated, tired, disappointed, etc. We should focus, not on the cause of the emotion, but on what it really is and admit those feelings to ourselves, God and others.

God wants us to grow in His grace and become spiritually mature. He wants us to become stronger and wiser. If every time we feel anger coming on, we reject it and replace it with the truth about what we are feeling we become more of what He wants us to be.

We want to be kind, but anger, or whatever the true emotion is, creates more of the same. Kindness flies out the window when someone makes us mad. If we can put a name to what we are really feeling and what caused it, we are more honest and can react with kindness.

When anger manifests as some other emotion, like sadness, we can say, "I am really sad." Once we have admitted the real emotion, it is easier to fix. When we are angry at someone, they usually get angry in return. When we say, "I am sad," the other person's response will normally be gentler. Anger is stopped.

Know this, my beloved brothers: let every person be quick to hear, slow to speak, slow to anger; for the anger of man

does not produce the righteousness of God (James 1: 19,20).

Our 'anger' is all about self, what we think we feel, what we want, or think we deserve. We are self-centered beings, and it is a constant struggle to see our true selves. If we realize our shortcomings, we can focus on Christ's example and react as He would react. How can we show the love of Christ to nonbelievers when we react with anger?

The Lord will fight for you, and you have only to be silent (Exodus 14:14).

Stopping anger is not in our power alone. We must call on the Holy Spirit to show us our true feelings so that we can deal with them. We can then approach the situation without hurting others, causing misunderstandings, getting into a fight, or doing all the things that tend to happen when people get angry.

But I say to you, love your enemies and pray for those who persecute you (Matthew 5:44).

Praying for those who persecute us or for those we think are persecuting us is not something we do naturally, but even short, terse prayers of "God bless them," will be honored by our Lord.

As we continue to pray, our own angry emotion and hurt will slowly fade away. We may never know what God does in the life of that person, but we will take a step closer to God. It is what He wants us to do; therefore, it is of value to us.

If we can apologize about a past angry confrontation, we should do it. We may save a friendship and could turn a life toward salvation. Being angry or right is not worth a soul.

Anger has never solved any problems. We can express what we are feeling, and why, without resorting to anger, with God's help.

Whoever is slow to anger has great understanding, but he who has a hasty temper exalts folly (Proverbs 14:29).

Prayer: **God, we ask today that you show us what we are really feeling and help us to react as your son Jesus would**

react. We want to be like you, hear your voice, and show your love to the world. We know that we have shown anger when we shouldn't have. Forgive us, Lord, and guide us each into kindness. Amen.

The World's Perceptions of Christians

Do not be surprised, brothers, that the world hates you (1 John 3:13).

Living and working among nonbelievers makes it difficult sometimes to be kind. Often, we try instead to fit in by keeping our Christianity to ourselves. We laugh at their jokes, join in their gossip, and even party with them, so they will think we are 'normal.' It is sad that many Christians feel they must do this.

The world judges Christians more harshly than any other religious group, atheists, or agnostics. Other religious groups do and wear whatever they want to schools and to work. They can close down streets to pray, but not Christians.

If we were to tell followers of other religions that they were prohibited from doing things important to them, we would be discriminating against them, but Christians can't pray in schools or put up Nativities in their towns (even though we are celebrating the birth of Christ). Christian private business owners cannot refuse to serve someone based on their beliefs even though other business owners can reserve the right to refuse service to anyone. We cannot afford unkindness.

Why are people unaware of this inequality? It is not a surprise. God told us that this would happen. The world is blind to the truth. Other religions are not a threat to the powers of darkness of this world because they are false. Their unkindness goes unnoticed by the world. Christianity is the one and only way to salvation, so the devil must do all he can to stop it.

We may not think people are watching us, but if we do one thing 'wrong' or 'politically incorrect' the world will criticize all Christianity. We are being judged on everything we do and everything we say. We must remember that we represent God.

We don't have to preach on the street corner to witness for Christ. Our very lives are being watched whether we know it or not. What we do and say will have an impact. It is imperative that we are kind if we are to make it a positive one.

In the same way, *let your light shine* before others, *so* that they may see your good works and give glory to your Father who is in heaven (Matthew 5:16).

Christians will always be persecuted, and part of our persecution is dealing with this type of prejudice, but we can't hide our light. We must tell our stories and always be open, above board, and honest in all our dealings.

If the world hates you, know that it has hated me before it hated you (John 15:18).

We are in a difficult place. If we allow ourselves to react as the world reacts, we will be criticized for not acting very 'Christian.' If we react with kindness, we are soft or unintelligent. If we react patiently with the truth, we are pushing our beliefs on others. There will be no praise from the world for reacting as God would like us to react. There will be no praise from the world for reacting as God would like us to react, and there will be no praise for reacting in a way God would not approve.

We will not ever be accepted by the world, but we must follow Christ's example no matter what. If we hide our Christianity from the world, we can't be a catalyst for change in those whose hearts God has prepared.

Indeed, all who desire to live a godly life in Christ Jesus will be persecuted (2 Timothy 3:12).

We in America may not suffer persecution like that in other countries. We are not thrown into jails, beaten, separated from our families, or killed…yet! But mistreatment for our beliefs is common, and that is why many of us are hiding them. We need to let our light shine.

For it is better to suffer for doing good, if that should be God's will, than for doing evil (1 Peter 3:17).

It is difficult to be kind when people around us are treating us badly for our beliefs, but kindness is the easiest way to show the world what true Christianity is about.

Prayer: **Father, help us to react with kindness and love when we receive ridicule for our beliefs. Keep us from vain arguments and religious disagreements that won't get us anywhere. Give us the words to say and guide our actions so that we always show your great love for all humankind. Amen.**

Spiritual Discernment

> **Beloved, do not believe every spirit, but test the spirits to see whether they are from God, for many false prophets have gone out into the world (1 John 4:1).**

Discernment:
1. The ability to judge well.
2. (In Christian contexts) Perception in the **absence of judgment** with a view of obtaining spiritual direction and understanding.

God speaks to us in many ways. Discernment is when God's Holy Spirit speaks to our hearts and tells us something is right or wrong. We all have moments in life when we just know in our hearts that something is off.

Sometimes we feel suddenly uncomfortable around a certain person or in a certain place. We might feel that someone is not being truthful. Others around might appear oblivious to what we are feeling.

> **The natural person does not accept the things of the Spirit of God, for they are folly to him, and he is not able to understand them because they are spiritually discerned (1 Corinthians 2:14).**

The Christian who has a strong relationship with God and listens to the leading of the Holy Spirit will find that some things in this world can only be spiritually discerned. The gift of discernment must go hand in hand with the fruit of kindness.

God's word says to discern without judgment. When we discern something is wrong, we can't just attack the person responsible. We may even have to allow the wrong to continue until such a time that we can, with Christian love, correct the wrong.

> **Do not judge by appearances, but judge with right judgment (John 7:24).**

Some people would explain discernment as listening to our 'gut.' We have a better sense of right and wrong because we have the Holy Spirit in our lives and as our influence, but it is more than that. God uses this gift to protect us from harm and from making mistakes.

The closer we draw to God and the more time we spend reading His word, the more discernment we will acquire. The more we listen to the Holy Spirit, the better we will be at discerning good from evil and right from wrong. The more discernment we have, the more kindness we will need.

> **And it is my prayer that your love may abound more and more, with knowledge and all discernment, so that you may approve what is excellent, and so be pure and blameless for the day of Christ (Philippians 1:9,10).**

Approving what is excellent among God's family is the main goal of discernment. Spiritual discernment will show us when teaching is incorrect or when the focus moves off Christ and to discussions and arguments about religiosity. With kindness, we are able to help lead teachings and discussions back to Christ.

> **But solid food is for the mature, for those who have their powers of discernment trained by constant practice to distinguish good from evil (Hebrews 5:14).**

Discernment is something that Christians develop over time through practice and prayer, being careful not to jump into something with both feet just because we 'feel' it. Not every **feeling** is discernment, and it is often not something we should share with others until we have spoken to God and made sure we are correct in His leading.

Some people may feel that they are just intuitive. Spiritual discernment relies on the knowledge of God's word and is available to all Christians. Discernment will never contradict God's word and will never encourage us to respond in a manner not befitting a Christian.

Greater discernment comes with training and practice. Intuition is just a feeling. If we believe we are discerning right from wrong, it is important to make sure it has a basis in scripture and is not based on our own feelings that day.

> **For the word of God is living and active, sharper than any two-edged sword, piercing to the division of soul and of spirit, of joints and of marrow, and discerning the thoughts and intentions of the heart (Hebrews 4:12).**

Discernment is not talked about much in churches today because it is so easily misunderstood and misused. However, it is very important and is mentioned in the Bible many times. It is a great tool for Christians to help lead us away from trouble and to where God wants us to go. It protects us from being taken in by false teachings and by people leading us astray about spiritual things.

As a gift from the Holy Spirit, discernment is available to all Christians. We need to ask for it and prayerfully consider all our 'gut' reactions to make sure they are from God and always react with kindness. Christ taught us not to judge. We look for spiritual directions and understanding without judgment.

Finally, just because we may discern something is wrong does not mean that we are to immediately try to fix or change it without much prayer. Knowledge before wisdom. Wisdom before discernment. Discernment only after much prayer and listening to the Holy Spirit. Pray for wisdom, and discernment will come.

> ***Prayer:*** **Oh Lord, send your Holy Spirit into our hearts to lead and guide us into your truth. Let us draw close to you so that we can hear what your Spirit says to us concerning all things. Amen.**

Do All to The Glory of God

So, whether you eat or drink, or whatever you do, do all to the glory of God. Give no offense to Jews or to Greeks or to the church of God, just as I try to please everyone in everything I do, not seeking my own advantage, but that of many, that they may be saved (1 Corinthians 10:31-33).

Daily, we make many choices. We choose when to get up, what to wear, what to eat, where to go, what to say, and so on. Is it possible to do all these things to the glory of God, not seeking our own advantage? If so, why would He care?

Some choices just make themselves. If we have pets or children, we feed them. We clean up and get dressed without any real conscious decisions being made except what colors go together. Thankfully, some of our decisions are not earth-shattering. Still, whatever we do is done for His glory because of our relationship with Him.

As we go through our day, we make decisions about how we should react to something someone has said or done. We decide if we are going to smile at the people around us, pull in front of that slow car, or eat the last brownie even though we know our spouse wants it. Must we be that kind? Doing all for God's glory is sometimes difficult.

What do we do when a situation arises where someone is mean to us, cheats us, or cuts us off in traffic? What can we do for the glory of God? We can be kind. Being kind is always for the glory of God. If nothing else, we can be kind.

We've heard the saying "no one knows what goes on behind closed doors." Maybe the unkind person's kids are addicts. Maybe they are deeply in debt, or secretly smoking, drinking, gambling, overeating and so on. Maybe they have health problems, or their parents are showing signs of Alzheimer's. They may look like they have it all together on the outside, but we can't really know. They need a little kindness.

For we are his workmanship, created in Christ Jesus for good works, which God prepared beforehand, that we should walk in them (Ephesians 2:10).

We will never regret doing the right thing. If we are alone and have an opportunity to cheat and we choose to do all for the glory of God, we will not cheat and will feel better because of our choice. We will not regret being honest. We will not regret repaying anger with kindness. We will not regret doing the right thing, but we will most definitely regret doing the wrong thing.

Prayer: **Lord, we want to do your will and, in everything we do, bring you glory. Help us to do the right things, the things that Christ would do, all the time. Thank you for your help. Amen.**

Should We Give to the Homeless?

Then the King will say to those on his right, 'Come, you who are blessed by my Father, inherit the kingdom prepared for you from the foundation of the world. For I was hungry, and you gave me food, I was thirsty and you gave me drink, I was a stranger and you welcomed me, I was naked and you clothed me, I was sick and you visited me, I was in prison and you came to me.' Then the righteous will answer him, saying, 'Lord, when did we see you hungry and feed you, or thirsty and give you drink? And when did we see you a stranger and welcome you, or naked and clothe you?'

The King will reply, 'Truly I tell you, whatever you did for one of the least of these brothers and sisters of mine, you did for me' (Matthew 25:34-40).

All over the country, we see homeless people pushing their carts or holding up a sign on every street corner asking for work, food or money. The signs are usually a variation on "Hungry anything helps," "will work for food," "Homeless veteran," etc.

Driving by these people is often uncomfortable, and having to stop at a stop light right next to them can cause us to look away. I feel that, as a Christian, we should give them something, but addicts in recovery tell me no. How can we be kind and at the same time not enable their addiction?

Some churches will make up what they call 'blessing bags' with toiletry items, food, socks, gloves, etc., to carry in their cars and give to those on the street. This is very positive for both the homeless person and the giver.

Working with the homeless, most of us find that they are very nice, grateful people who are struggling with life issues. Some have addictions, some don't. Some have mental illnesses, and some don't. Some will take advantage of our kindness, but some are truly interested in making a positive change in their lives. Sounds just like the rest of the world.

To find those who are seriously interested in making better life decisions and taking steps to improve their lives and possibly accepting the Lord, we must work with the homeless, establishing relationships until we have developed trust.

If we feel that we are being taken advantage of, that is okay. We have shown kindness and may never know how that will affect them later in life. At least those people will have something to eat and something to wear. When we find one who is sincere, it can be counted as a blessing. We often gain more from them than they do from us.

Whoever is generous to the poor lends to the Lord, and he will repay him for his deed (Proverbs 19:17).

It is important to understand that many of the homeless are not there because of anything under their control. Many have no family, were raised in foster care, have no skills, or have a disability. Many have become dependent on pain medication that is no longer available.

We may wonder why they don't just get it together and rent an apartment or go to a shelter. The truth is that shelters are often full, or the person doesn't meet their criteria. Apartments require background checks that cost money and often can't be passed. Hotels need driver's licenses, and many of the homeless' licenses have expired due to lack of funds.

It may seem simple to us, but it is more difficult than we think. Family relationship bridges have often been burned by addicts, and they are not welcome even when they get clean. Hopelessness is a serious disease among the homeless. They need our kindness more than anyone.

Whoever closes his ear to the cry of the poor will himself call out and not be answered (Proverbs 21:13).

Kindness helps people who feel hopeless. We can open our hearts and minds and tamp down our judgmental nature. The old saying "There, but for the grace of God, go I" applies when we see the homeless in our communities.

If we think there is nothing we can do, we are wrong. If we have no food or blessing bag to give, we can pray, we can smile, we can listen, and we can be kind.

This short poem was written by a man without a home:

Look into our eyes,
see how tired we are,
listen to our life stories,
bless our hearts.
For what we, the homeless (the unseen and unknown)
need is a place to keep warm and dry at night,
a dollar or two for a cup of hot coffee
or getting the next meal.
Even a few minutes talking to someone
can bring a smile to our hearts.
Lance Kearns

Prayer: **Lord, let us see our neighbors who are homeless and realize that they may also feel hopeless. Send us where you need us. Show us how to care. Let us remember that these are people just like us and that you love them and died for them. You want them in your kingdom. Amen.**

We Don't Feel Like Being Kind

Be angry and do not sin; do not let the sun go down on your anger (Ephesians 4:26).

If we are honest with ourselves, and with God, we must admit that sometimes we don't like the people we love. They make us angry. They are irritating, frustrating and, in our opinions at that time, just not too bright. We don't feel like being kind at these times.

Sometimes, kindness is easier with strangers than with family and friends. Even though we love these people, occasionally our patience and love are to the breaking point.

These feelings can come out of nowhere. The culprit could be the weather or something we ate. Whatever it is, the devil will use it to make us and others miserable. He will use it to make us unkind and to draw us away from the joy God wants us to have in our lives and families. When we don't feel like being kind, we also aren't happy or joyful.

The Holy Spirit is always with us, but we turn our backs on Him and allow negative feelings to overtake us. God wants us to be kind to each other, but we find ourselves in a human place that makes us crabby, hateful, sarcastic, or depressed.

Hatred stirs up strife, but love covers all offenses (Proverbs 10:12).

These feelings, although normal, can cause all kinds of problems if we don't identify the cause and make a conscious effort to fight against them. We know that whomever we are frustrated with probably doesn't know what they did or didn't do, and they probably didn't do it on purpose. There usually is a 'last straw' that puts us over the edge into unkindness. It can be a very confusing time for everyone.

We can handle these situations in a multitude of ways. We can criticize, cry, yell, fight, or avoid conflict altogether. We can throw up our hands and give up trying. We can cause hurt and be unkind.

These are not the best ways to deal with times of stress and strife in relationships and is not the kindness that God has provided for us and that He wants us to produce in our lives.

Writing down what we are feeling and what caused them can give us insight and strength to resist our human need to strike out. Taking a break from the other person (not storming out in anger) can be a good idea if we have difficulty allowing God to take control.

> **Let no corrupting talk come out of your mouths, but only such as is good for building up, as fits the occasion, that it may give grace to those who hear (Ephesians 4:29).**

Building each other up, even when we don't feel like it, is the truest form of kindness. This kindness can cost us, and we may not like it. Even though we know the negative feelings will go away in time, kindness is still difficult.

The Holy Spirit can help us be kind and avoid worsening the situation until the unkind feelings pass. Prayer works. The Holy Spirit has not gone away, and we can trust the Lord to control our tongues and our actions, if we let Him.

Kindness from the Holy Spirit can hasten the passing of negative feelings. Kindness fights the devil. Kindness creates a good environment that breeds more kindness. Kindness is not just a fruit we use with strangers or people from church. Being kind to family and friends is not only more difficult, but more valuable.

> *Prayer:* **Lord, help us to be kind even when things are not going our way. Even when we are frustrated, infuse our tongues and hearts with kindness for those around us. Help us to be fair to others, knowing that whatever they have done is probably more our problem than theirs. Thank you for being kind to us even when we frustrate you. Amen.**

Unity of the Body of Christ

Do nothing from rivalry or conceit, but in humility count others more significant than yourselves (Philippians 2:3).

Unity among the body of Christ is very important yet often difficult. If the body is in disarray, we are not able to accomplish what God has set before us, which is reaching the lost. The body is always called to be kind and to encourage each member to work for the Lord with the talents and skills that He has given them.

We can also encourage those who are shy or ignoring their gifts, by getting them to join us in projects until they become confident and know what God is asking of them.

As a prisoner for the Lord, then, I urge you to live a life worthy of the calling you have received. Be completely humble and gentle; be patient, bearing with one another in love. Make every effort to keep the unity of the Spirit through the bond of peace. There is one body and one Spirit, just as you were called to one hope when you were called; one Lord, one faith, one baptism; one God and Father of all, who is over all and through all and in all (Ephesians 4:1-6 NIV).

Bearing one another in love and unity means we, as members of the body of Christ, are kind to all other members, knowing that we are all different. We have all received God's call. He knocked at our doors until we answered, and we accepted His truth and the gift of His Son.

Once we accepted God's call to salvation, we all became part of the body of Christ, but we did not all become the same. We maintained our individuality and our talents or gifts.

Some also received special callings such as preaching, teaching, and the ability and desire to spend time in prayer. We all have strengths in various areas, and we are all different. Even though we may not see or do things alike, we are kind to those who are doing things differently.

And he gave some, apostles; and some, prophets; and some, evangelists; and some, pastors and teachers; For the perfecting of the saints, for the work of the ministry, for the edifying of the body of Christ (Ephesians 4:11-12).

God will encourage us at times to do things outside our comfort zone if they need to be done and there is no one else, but the body runs more smoothly if everyone does what they are good at doing and no one tries to micro-manage another's efforts for the Lord.

Our gifts stay with us, even though we may use them in different ways or on different projects. It is difficult for us to understand that not everything has to be done the way we would do it. We need to use the gifts that we have been given, and let others do what God has called them to do.

If we are not using our gifts—whatever it is that God has given us the desire and ability to do—they will still be there whether we use the gift or not. It may take time to discover what our abilities and callings are from God, but in our walk with Him, our gifts will become clear.

Eager to maintain the unity of the Spirit in the bond of peace (Ephesians 4:3).

If the differences among us affect church unity, we are not doing what God has asked, or we are not letting each other use the talents we have been given. Are we making some members feel as if they don't have any gifts or callings? Is there envy or discouragement? Are some of the members developing pride because of their special gifts or are they looking down on those who aren't participating in church projects? Church unity takes special kindness to maintain.

God gave gifts to us so we could help build His kingdom and encourage each other. We are to help spread the Good News, to build up one another, to bear each other's burdens, and to commune with Him.

So, if there is any encouragement in Christ, any comfort from love, any participation in the Spirit, any affection and sympathy, complete my joy by being of the same mind, having the same love, being in full accord and of one mind (Philippians 2:1).

None of us are without fault. No one's gift is so great that other gifts are not needed. Let God take each person through their own learning process to find what He wants of them. Be kind and bear one another's burdens. Restore those who are discouraged.

> **Finally, brothers, rejoice. Aim for restoration, comfort one another, agree with one another, live in peace; and the God of love and peace will be with you (2 Corinthians 13:11).**

Prayer: **Lord, give us unity among the members of your body, no matter what church we attend. Let us come together in prayer and worship, encouraging one another. Individually, show us the strengths and gifts you have given us and show us how and when to use them. Let us always be kind to others who are in a different place on your path. Amen.**

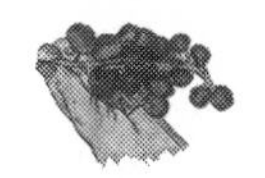

Goodness:
The sixth fruit of the Holy Spirit

> **But the fruit of the Spirit is love, joy, peace, patience, kindness, goodness, faithfulness, gentleness, and self-control. Against such things there is no Law. And those who belong to Christ Jesus have crucified the flesh with its passions and desires. If we live by the Spirit, let us also keep in step with the Spirit (Galatians 5:22-25).**

Goodness is a quality that requires an effort from us. Goodness helps us choose right from wrong and to resist evil. Goodness makes us choose God's way as our path.

There are four main words for goodness, one in the Old Testament, *tob*, and three in the New Testament, *kalos, agathos*, or *chrestos*.

The words have common meanings when used to describe items, such as a tree, i.e., the tree is good. These words also are used to express moral attributes when talking about God's goodness or when saying the Lord is good.

Our human goodness comes from God's goodness and involves positive behavior and traits. God is good to us; therefore, we are good to others.

> **Be perfect, therefore, as your heavenly Father is perfect (Matthew 5:48 NIV).**

The God of Goodness

Oh, how abundant is your goodness, which you have stored up for those who fear you and worked for those who take refuge in you, in the sight of the children of mankind! (Psalm 31:19).

God is good. He is the only one who is truly good. His goodness towards us reaches into every part of our lives. We believe that everything in our lives will be all right, even if it doesn't turn out the way we want it to. We believe that everything happens for a reason, and that reason is to bring the world to know Him.

Here is a bothersome recent Facebook post by an unknown person:

> *"I do not believe that everything in my life will necessarily be all right and I certainly do not believe that everything happens for a reason. I believe that whatever kind of God exists is the kind of God who can't or won't interfere every time humans decide to do horrible things to each other, because humans are clearly doing terrible things to each other every day and show very few signs of stopping."*

Our nature is sinful. Our fall from grace due to free will in the garden created this reality. Also, this world has laws of nature that God put into place, like gravity. If we jump off a 40-story building, we are going to fall to our death. If we drive 200 miles an hour around a sharp corner, we are also probably going to die. If a large board falls on our head, it is going to hurt. These are laws of nature that God put into place.

God does not cause these bad things to happen. Only good things come from God. However, we cannot expect bad things to be suspended for Christians or for anyone who pleads with God.

For he makes his sun rise on the evil and on the good and sends rain on the just and on the unjust (Matthew 5:45b).

Consequently, we know that world is made up of sinful people with free will, and we live with the unchangeable laws of nature. This combination has produced a world today where bad things happen to everyone.

God is not a fairy godmother who will wave His wand and set all things right. That would take away free will, the consequences of sin, and the laws of nature. When nonbelievers ask why bad things happen, we need to remember these reasons.

People in the world are doing terrible things to each other, and although God is good, He will not interfere with our free will. Christians, though not of this world, will still have bad things happen to them. The laws of nature apply to us, but we have the goodness of God to get us through bad times. We know that He will make good come out of the bad things that happen for those of us who love Him.

We believe that God created us to fellowship with Him and to be His children. Even though some have turned their backs on Him, He still wants that relationship with everyone. He stands at the door and knocks and knocks—every door, every person, everywhere, all the time. And our final reward is eternal life with Him.

If eternal life were all we got out of this, that would be good enough. Anything that happens in our very short lives is nothing compared to eternity with God. However, because God is good, there is more to this life than just waiting for eternity.

> **Every good gift and every perfect gift is from above, coming down from the Father of lights with whom there is no variation or shadow due to change (James 1:17).**

Because God is working in our lives and in the lives of the lost, we can say that everything does happen for a reason. We may not always see the results of our prayers or the good that is produced from our challenges, but we do have the Holy Spirit to enrich our lives. He gives us peace and joy in addition to God's goodness.

With the Holy Spirit living through us, we can show the fruit of goodness in our own lives. During this life, God has promised us goodness through His Holy Spirit, no matter what terrible things are happening.

> ***Prayer*: God, your goodness to us is a great gift. We understand how this world works and we do not blame you when bad things happen. We love you and thank you that you are always with us and working for our good. Let our goodness to others also be a gift from you. Amen.**

Good Fruit in Words

> **"Either make the tree good and its fruit good, or make the tree bad and its fruit bad, for the tree is known by its fruit. You brood of vipers! How can you speak good, when you are evil? For out of the abundance of the heart the mouth speaks. The good person out of his good treasure brings forth good, and the evil person out of his evil treasure brings forth evil. I tell you, on the day of judgment people will give account for every careless word they speak, for by your words you will be justified, and by your words you will be condemned" (Matthew 12:33-27).**

We are sometimes a careless people. We are careless with our actions towards others. We are careless in our responsibilities, and we are careless with our words in person and in writing. We are known by what we say and what we write. People don't know our thoughts, but they know what we put out there for all to see.

We may think no one notices when we are careless with our written words. Those faceless beings out in social media land don't care what we write, do they? Yes, they do, and our words are often hurtful. Our words can lead people away from God. Our words can affect how people view Christianity.

God also notices and cares about our carelessness. How can we be filled with goodness if our words are evil or causing pain to others? Either make the tree *good* or make the tree *bad.*

God is the only one who is truly good, and all good things come from Him. He cannot be evil. He cannot speak evil or do evil. He is good, and there is only good that comes from Him. If we profess to follow Him, then only goodness should come from our actions and our words.

Our hearts are hardened by evil, and being good is difficult for us because this world is evil. God knows that we cannot be good on our own, so He has provided a way for us in the Holy Spirit. The more we practice goodness, the easier it will become.

Showing God's goodness in our words requires that we think before we speak, and truly listen to other's needs before we act. Often, not responding at all to what we read is the best course of action, particularly if what we read or our response will be negative.

Before we were saved, when we were still the 'old man' and not a new creation, we reacted emotionally before thinking or listening. This world moves at a fast pace, and it is sometimes all we can do to keep up with our daily lives. How can we find the time to think before we speak? Thank God, through the Holy Spirit, we can.

> **Who is wise and understanding among you? By his good conduct let him show his works in the meekness of wisdom (James 3:13).**

We are also a selfish people, drawn away by our own wants and needs. We ask God for everything under the sun, but we forget to ask Him to help us be good to others and protect the words that come from our mouths and the words that we write.

When we get on social media, we write whatever comes to mind. We respond to others' posts. Our thoughts come fast and furious. We need to stop and reread what we have written before hitting that post button.

What is in our hearts is what will create goodness. Only if we are reading, hearing, and believing God's word and His teaching will goodness come. If we are surrounding ourselves with evil writings, arguments, dirty jokes, unnecessary photos, and the like, we will not produce goodness. If we spend more time on social media than we do in God's word, what we see and learn on social media is what will be in our hearts.

God is the center of our lives, nothing else. Having Jesus Christ in our hearts and having a relationship with Him that is close and strong is what will produce goodness from our mouths and our actions.

> **Let love be genuine. Abhor what is evil; hold fast to what is good (Romans 12:9).**

Evil constantly moves around us, and we abhor it, but we look at it day after day. It creeps into our hearts, and out of our hearts, our words reflect evil. A person who surrounds themselves with bad will have a difficult time being good. We need to fight to keep the old man under submission daily.

True goodness that comes from a good heart is not simple. We know this because we all fail. Our God forgives us, but we still must continually call upon His Holy Spirit for goodness to dwell in our hearts, so that what comes out of our hearts is the goodness that He desires.

***Prayer:* Lord, let us always react with goodness and show your goodness to the world around us. We know that the only way for us to have goodness in our hearts is to have you in our hearts. We thank you and praise you for your Son Jesus, who has given us your Holy Spirit and the goodness He provides. Amen.**

How Big Is Your Needle?

All scripture is from Matthew 19:16-26.

Just then, a man came up to Jesus and inquired, "Teacher, what good thing must I do to obtain eternal life?"

"Why do you ask Me about what is good?" Jesus replied, "There is only One who is good. If you want to enter life, keep the commandments."

"Which ones?" the man asked.

Jesus answered, "'Do not murder, do not commit adultery, do not steal, do not bear false witness, honor your father and mother, and love your neighbor as yourself.'"

Before Jesus' death and resurrection, the New Covenant had not been established. When this man came to Jesus for answers, he is told to obey the commandments of the law, which he had always done. Jesus also pointed out that only God is truly good.

The man who was asking Jesus these questions was wealthy, and he desired eternal life with Christ, but He had a flaw that Jesus saw that the others could not see. He loved his riches more than he desired eternal life. He trusted his riches more than He trusted Christ.

"All these I have kept," said the young man. "What do I still lack?"

Jesus told him, "If you want to be perfect, go, sell your possessions and give to the poor, and you will have treasure in heaven. Then come, follow Me."

When the young man heard this, he went away in sorrow, because he had great wealth.

We don't know if he ever came back or if he did what Jesus asked of him. We hope that he did, but his attitude exists in many today. People blessed with money (not all wealthy people, by any means), trust in their riches more than they trust in God, and have great difficulty giving to those in need and following Him.

Then Jesus said to His disciples, "Truly I tell you, it is difficult for a rich man to enter the kingdom of heaven. Again, I tell you, it is easier for a camel to pass through the eye of a needle than for a rich man to enter the kingdom of God."

Often, those of us who do not have great wealth wonder why someone, maybe a family member or friend who is wealthy, is not helping us. They have so much, and we have so little. They see us struggling, and yet they don't help and sometimes don't even realize how blessed they are.

This can frustrate those who are struggling financially, to the point that they may turn away from these people and from God.

If they are not believers, then the trust they have placed in money as their security is not totally their fault. The devil has blinded their eyes so that they see only their own needs and wants. They don't trust God, they trust in money. They are proud of what they have and feel deserving of this wealth. It is the powers of darkness that are blocking the way for them to see the truth of God's goodness and love.

As believers in God, most wealthy become generous, and God's goodness is in them.

Only God, who is good, can bring the others into His kingdom. Once someone knows the Lord, they would never give up their Christian lives, struggles and all, for the riches in this world.

We have more than they will ever have if they don't find the truth and follow Him. We have eternal life with Christ. We have the assurance that God will meet our needs. Looking back, we can see that He always has met our needs and, looking forward, we know that He always will. Christ gives us a generous spirit so we can help others, and we get to experience the joy of doing so.

Others may have money, and they fear life without it. They work diligently at holding on to it. They miss the blessings of God. They die in their sins. We must pray for these people, that their eyes are opened, and for ourselves, that we will have greater faith in our good God.

We must see them for the lost souls they are and have compassion, not jealousy, hate or anger. Pray that they learn the truth, ask Christ into their lives and use their wealth for the good of the kingdom. With God all things are possible.

When the disciples heard this, they were greatly astonished and asked, "Who then can be saved?"

Jesus looked at them and said, "With man this is impossible, but with God all things are possible" (Matthew 19:16-26).

Prayer: **Lord, help us to pray for all the lost in this world who don't know you and your goodness, especially those who have great wealth. Let us have faith in your blessings and a certainty that you will meet our needs. Let us remember that you are all we need, not the riches of this world. Amen.**

The Future is Now

For the grace of God has appeared, bringing salvation for all people, training us to renounce ungodliness and worldly passions, and to live self-controlled, upright, and godly lives in the present age, waiting for our blessed hope, the appearing of the glory of our great God and Savior Jesus Christ, who gave himself for us to redeem us from all lawlessness and to purify for himself a people for his own possession who are zealous for good works (Titus 2:11-14).

Often, we believe that we do not know enough and are not good enough to be used by God for His good works. We think we should wait until later when we know more and feel ready. Sometime in the future, we will be able to work for the Lord.

God wants us to know that the future is *now*. Salvation is available *now* to everyone. And for those of us who are saved by grace, He wants us to work for His kingdom *now*. We will never **feel** that we are ready and according to scripture, we never will **be** good enough.

In time, if we study, we will become more knowledgeable, but God wants to use us *now*. None of us are guaranteed tomorrow, so we need to serve now, or we may miss our chance, and we will miss out on being blessed for our service. Worst of all, someone may die without hearing of God's goodness and salvation.

God has a plan, and He needs us to help carry it out. If we don't do it, who will? Almost everyone we know is insecure in some way and doesn't feel ready to witness or do God's work. But His burden is light, and He will not ask us to do anything for which we are unprepared.

But be doers of the word, and not hearers only, deceiving yourselves (James 1:22).

Being doers of the word doesn't sound that difficult. But God's word says a lot of things like 'love your neighbor as you love yourself' which can at times prove difficult. Then we are instructed to 'pray for those who persecute you.' Being doers of the word is harder than it sounds.

If we are doers and not hearers only, that implies that we need to hear the word to do it. So, we need to read the Bible, listen to sermons, and pray. Then we need to act on the word of God and live according to the word. This is one way we can do God's work.

> **Do your best to present yourself to God as one approved, a worker who has no need to be ashamed, rightly handling the word of truth (2 Timothy 2:15).**

We can see that what God requires of us is to show the world His love and demonstrate what it means to follow Him through our lives. We are to let our light shine in a very dark world by showing His goodness through our goodness.

> **And God is able to make all grace abound to you, so that having all sufficiency in all things at all times, you may abound in every good work (2 Corinthians 9:8).**

God will enable us when the time is right for us to serve. The Bible explains that living in the world is not all about us. It is about others and letting them know that God loves them (and us) just as we are now.

We won't get more comfortable serving God without drawing closer to God. Our service is worthless without God. People will not come to know God on their own. It is our responsibility to share the good news to the world by our love, our attitudes, our words, our reactions, our goodness, and our lives.

If we are honest with ourselves, we know that fear is what stops us from working for the Lord. We also know where this fear comes from. We must resist the devil and force ourselves to move forward.

The devil makes us think that working for God is difficult and that someone else, more qualified will do it. We don't know the scriptures well enough, we don't like confrontations, we don't speak well, and many other excuses. But here are some ways we can help God with His plan of salvation for those around us.

Instead of fearing about not knowing all the scripture from memory, we can speak only about our own experiences. Nonbelievers will know we are different by our lifestyle and they will be curious.

Using our own experiences to tell them about Christ is the easiest way to speak out. We don't need to answer any deep religious questions. We can just tell them how Jesus changed our lives. We can tell them about our relationship with the Lord.

> **If any of you lacks wisdom, let him ask God, who gives generously to all without reproach, and it will be given him (James 1:5).**

If we live by the word of the Lord, we will not fail in showing our light to the world. God will give us wisdom when situations arise where there is an opportunity to show His love. We may not always see the results of living our lives for Him, and we may not think that anything was accomplished at all, but we are certain that God is working in every situation to bring the lost into His loving arms.

Living our lives for God will bless others, and we may be surprised at how God uses whatever service we offer Him. God wants to use us and will bless us for doing His work. Don't make Him find someone else and don't make Him wait for the future.

> **Submit yourselves therefore to God. Resist the devil, and he will flee from you (James 4:7).**

> ***Prayer:*** **Lord, let my lifestyle reflect your word so that when you need me, I am ready to tell your story. Cast out my fear with your love. Help me to show your goodness in every situation. Amen.**

Relationship Over Religion

For the time is coming when people will not endure sound teaching but having itching ears they will accumulate for themselves teachers to suit their own passions and will turn away from listening to the truth and wander off into myths. As for you, always be sober-minded, endure suffering, do the work of an evangelist, fulfill your ministry (2 Timothy 4:5).

Many of us were raised in 'a church.' We may have attended what would be called a 'nominal' church, a place where people go to hear what they want to hear and not what God wants them to hear.

Nominal means 'in name only.' Nominal Christians are Christians in name only. They identify with a church or denomination, but it doesn't require any morality or lifestyle change. Some are 'good' people, they just don't have a personal relationship with Jesus. They will not endure sound teaching because it requires more than they are willing to give.

Many nominal Christians claim the title of Christ but belong to a church that is more of a social club, perhaps doing good works, going to meetings, following church rules, etc. However, they are not hearing the truth and, therefore, are not enjoying a true bond with God the Father. They are missing out on the goodness of God, and they are living life as if He didn't exist in any real way.

Christianity is more than a title and more than just attending church. Christianity is a relationship of the heart with Christ, who died for our sins and rose from the dead. He gave us His Holy Spirit to guide us and help us in this life as we commune with Him.

We know from our earthly friends what having a relationship is like. If we don't spend as much time with Christ as we do with them, talking, laughing, asking for support, trusting and bringing our struggles to Him, we do not have much of a relationship. But He is good and is patiently waiting for us to come closer.

If you declare with your mouth, "Jesus is Lord," and believe in your heart that God raised him from the dead, you will be saved. For it is with your heart that you

> **believe and are justified, and it is with your mouth that you profess your faith and are saved (Romans 10:9-10 NIV).**

If a church never mentions salvation, relationship, being born again, giving our hearts to the Lord, or asking Him to forgive our sins, it is a 'nominal' church, and we are missing out on, not only salvation, but a great friend.

If someone tells us that we have never done anything bad enough for God to send us to hell, we know we are talking to the wrong people. They do not understand the plan of salvation and why Christ died and rose again.

God is good. He does not send anyone to hell. God has provided a way for us to have eternal life with Him. Jesus died in our place for the sins of the world. All we must do is accept this gift, ask forgiveness of our sins, and start a relationship with Him.

Being 'good enough' is not required to accept the Lord into our hearts. We never will be. He died for us while we were still sinners. We cannot be fooled. Not everyone will go to heaven, no matter how 'good' they are. A belief and relationship with Christ is the only way. Religion alone will not get us there.

> **For by grace you have been saved through faith. And this is not your own doing; it is the gift of God, not a result of works, so that no one may boast (Ephesians 2:8,9).**

We have a free choice to either accept that Christ died for our sins and follow Him, or not. We choose where we will spend eternity, and it is not by our good works that we get into heaven. It is not by attending church or belonging to a denomination.

Some churches teach that to go to heaven, being a good person is all it takes. This is heartbreaking. How can we reach people for Christ when they already think they are Christians?

It is not ours to judge whether a person has a personal relationship with Christ by their outward behavior. We can only pray for those we are unsure of, that they do have that relationship with our Lord. We can take opportunities to talk about Christ's death on the cross and make sure they understand what being a Christian is all about.

Being ready always to explain the difference between religion and relationship is a must. Many people are against 'organized' religion and religiosity. We can show and tell them about Jesus, our brother and friend.

We know that God looks on a person's heart. As Christians with a personal relationship with the Lord, we want others to know the truth and have the same type of relationship. We can also show what a relationship with Christ is by living our lives for Him.

> **And to the angel of the church in Sardis write: 'The words of him who has the seven spirits of God and the seven stars. I know your works. You have the reputation of being alive, but you are dead' (Revelation 3:1).**

The Lord wants us to gather together to worship Him. Attending a Bible-believing church gives us strength. We need to look closely at the church's teaching and our reasons for attending. We want to follow Christ's example and do good works, but we can't rely on them for our salvation.

Listening closely to the preaching in our churches for teachings on salvation and believing that the Bible is the word of God are two ways we will know if we are where God wants us. We can ensure that we are not nominal Christians attending a nominal church that is full of the bondage of man's rules.

> **Not everyone who says to Me, 'Lord, Lord,' shall enter the kingdom of heaven, but he who does the will of My Father in heaven. Many will say to Me in that day, 'Lord, Lord, have we not prophesied in Your name, cast out demons in Your name, and done many wonders in Your name?' And then I will declare to them, 'I never knew you; depart from Me, you who practice lawlessness! (Matthew 7:21-23 NKJV).**

God will not allow works in His name to fail even if the person doing them is doing them from a wrong spirit. We may think we are doing all kinds of great things for God, but if He doesn't know us (which means we don't know Him), those works will not lead to our salvation.

Prayer: **Heavenly Father, strengthen our relationship with you and don't let us be drawn into religious emptiness. Open our eyes to your truth and goodness and lead us to attend true churches that teach your word and help our relationship with your grow. Amen.**

No One Really Knows

Oh, taste and see that the Lord is good! Blessed is the man who takes refuge in him! (Psalms 34:8).

Sometimes we are very strange. We become so used to hiding our struggles that we even try to hide them from God. We forget that we can take refuge in Him. We forget to lay our burdens at the foot of the cross and leave them there for Him to deal with. When we do lay them down, our lack of trust causes us to pick them up repeatedly and pretend that all is well.

We often hide our burdens from our Christian brothers and sisters. We want to seem as if we have no troubles in this life and we are 'good' Christians. We don't want anyone to know.

We make our lives more difficult than they need be in Christ. We react to our problems the same as we did before Christ came into our hearts. We worry about things we have no control over. We try to change things that we cannot change and that may be, in fact, none of our business.

Instead of allowing God to work in us and do what needs doing, we jump in to try to fix things and cause ourselves a great deal of stress. We worry, worry, worry and yet want to seem as 'good' Christians, with no problems, wise and calm amid the stormy sea.

What is man, that he can be pure? Or he who is born of a woman, that he can be righteous? (Job 15:14).

If we take our burdens to the Lord and share them with our Christian brothers and sisters, we can become wise and calm. Where the world struggles and becomes angry, we are good and loving. Because of God's goodness in us, we can show light to the world instead of darkness and calm instead of panic. We can have rest and peace.

...for the fruit of light is found in all that is good and right and true (Ephesians 5:9).

Those who have known the Lord for a long time may appear to have it more together than the rest of us, but the only difference between a mature Christian and a new Christian is how much they allow Christ to be the center of their lives.

Mature Christians have developed a deep trust in His care and divine goodness. What they don't realize is the good that could come if they would share their past struggles, experiences, and the hope they have in God. This information could be a great help and comfort to those who are hiding their problems.

We can pretend that all is well, and no one will ever need to know. We can go on struggling and pretending. Is this what God wants for His children?

Keeping our struggles to ourselves and not joining together with other Christians will certainly mean that everyone will think we are perfect, but it will also ensure that we will not grow in the Lord or be of help to anyone else. No one will come to us for help if we don't seem to have any problems of our own.

Christianity is not about looking flawless or impressing others; it is about loving God, loving others, bearing each other's burdens and allowing the body of Christ to know our struggles so that we can build each other up.

Prayer: **God you are good. You care for us, and you know what our struggles and problems are and that we do not have it all together, but you love us anyway. Help us to show what is going on in our lives when doing so will help others to grow in their relationship with you. Amen.**

Pride, the Good, the Bad, and the Ugly

When pride comes, then comes disgrace, but with the humble is wisdom (Proverbs 11:2).

When does pride become a problem? Is it wrong to be proud of our accomplishments? Is it wrong to be proud of our children? It is acceptable to be proud of others and of ourselves for accomplishing what God has helped us accomplish. He gives us a lot of good things to be proud of.

The pride that causes problems for us is the pride that says we are better than anyone else, that everyone should listen to us, or that our ways are the only ways. Pride is a sin when we want people to respect us more than they respect God. It is when we feel that we deserve recognition for all the great things we have done or said, or for how we look. When we believe that we have accomplished everything on our own without God, then there is a problem.

In the early 1980s, some schools began a program for kindergarten children to develop self-esteem. On paper, it looked great. Each child was given a mirror and told to look at themselves and say, "you are the most important person in the world."

Did this build self-esteem or cause something much worse? Children do need to feel good about themselves, to believe that they are equal to other children and loved by God. However, this created a prideful, self-centered generation who are now seeking their own satisfaction above all else.

Do nothing out of selfish ambition or empty pride, but in humility consider others more important than yourselves (Philippians 2:3).

The Bible says to think of others as better than ourselves. This is the true goodness of God. However, it is not natural for us to think of others as more important, and if we do, it is sometimes in a negative way that makes us jealous or feel bad about ourselves. That is not God's intent. God wants us to put others first, out of a heart filled with His goodness, caring for others, showing the goodness of God in our own lives and actions. Our satisfaction and joy come from putting others before ourselves.

If we are of the generation that grew up thinking the opposite—that we are better than everyone else—we need to read God's word and adjust our thinking. We should not look at the world or at God and ask, 'what's in it for me?' Instead, we should consider what God wants us to do for others and for Him.

Goodness is a level of maturity in Christians and is different from all the other fruit of the spirit, even kindness. Goodness is internal, and is not a natural state of humanity. Goodness needs to be practiced, not as good deeds (although those are wonderful), but as an essential state of being. There is no sinful pride when God is central.

Satan existed as an angel of God. He was originally wise and completely righteous. However, pride caused Satan to fall, since he wanted to receive the worship due to God alone.

> **You were an anointed guardian cherub. I placed you; you were on the holy mountain of God; in the midst of the stones of fire you walked. You were blameless in your ways from the day you were created, till unrighteousness was found in you. In the abundance of your trade you were filled with violence in your midst, and you sinned; so I cast you as a profane thing from the mountain of God, and I destroyed you, O guardian cherub, from the midst of the stones of fire. Your heart was proud because of your beauty; you corrupted your wisdom for the sake of your splendor. I cast you to the ground; I exposed you before kings, to feast their eyes on you (Ezekiel 28:14-17).**

Satan allowed the goodness of God to leave His heart because he thought he was better than his creator. He became proud and arrogant. When we see ourselves as great in our own eyes, pride drives out our God-given goodness.

> **When pride comes, then comes disgrace, but with the humble is wisdom (Proverbs 11:2).**

We must remember that all we have, all we know, all we do comes from God. We should rather have wisdom than disgrace and be humble instead of prideful. Let us strive to give God the glory and not ourselves.

Prayer: **Father in heaven, please take sinful pride away from us. Let us remember that without you we are nothing. Help us show the world your loving kindness and goodness and put others before ourselves with joy. Amen.**

We Are Good Enough

For all have sinned and fall short of the glory of God (Romans 3:23).

So often we feel 'less than' those around us. We believe that others are smarter, better looking, more dedicated, better Christians, have more friends, not lazy, have cleaner houses, better families and relationships, etc.

We may feel we are not good enough to come before God with our requests or even to invite Him into our lives and have a relationship. We don't believe we are good enough for God, and we are right. We never will be. But He wants us anyway.

We look at others and think that they are good enough, and that is what we want. Interestingly, what we see and think about them is not the whole story. What we see and think about them is the same as what they see and think about us. None of us are worthy of God, and we are unable to judge another's worthiness by what we see on the outside.

When we feel that we are not good enough, we think we can't ask God for His favor. When deep down we think we don't deserve any blessings, we will stop praying altogether.

But the truth is that we can come before God and ask for His favor, because He told us we can. He told us that "all have fallen short of His glory, "and He told us to "bring our needs before Him."

For Christians who feel unworthy, God says we are forgiven, so we are worthy. For those who haven't committed their lives to God or asked Christ into their hearts yet, God says everyone sins, everyone falls short, He loves us just as we are and wants us to come to Him now. He doesn't want us to wait, thinking we are not good enough. We aren't, and the goodness of God is that He loves and wants us anyway.

I do not understand what I do. For what I want to do I do not do, but what I hate I do. And if I do what I do not want to do, I agree that the law is good. As it is, it is no longer I myself who do it, but it is sin living in me. For I know that good itself does not dwell in me, that is, in my sinful nature. For I have the desire to do what is good, but I cannot

> **carry it out. For I do not do the good I want to do, but the evil I do not want to do—this I keep on doing. Now if I do what I do not want to do, it is no longer I who do it, but it is sin living in me that does it (Romans 7:15-20).**

Remember the apostles that Jesus called. None of them were good enough. One was a hated tax collector. We are important to God, and He created us as we are. We need to come to Him with our needs, confess our sins so that He can forgive them, and then we can forgive ourselves.

God loves us. He wants us to come to Him with everything. He has good plans for us when we follow Him. In a sense, we are not good enough, but in His eyes, we are good enough to come as we are and be forgiven. Christ died for us while we were yet sinners.

> **There is therefore now no condemnation for those who are in Christ Jesus (Romans 8:1).**

All we know is that with God, life is much more joyful, and without Him, it is an empty struggle day after day. God's goodness is what makes us good enough.

> **As it is written: "None is righteous, no, not one" (Romans 3:10).**

> ***Prayer:*** **Lord, we know that only you are truly good. Help us not to feel ourselves as unworthy to come before you with our worship and our needs. Let us hear your heart and feel your love. Let us know that you want us, you care for us, and you died because you loved us so much. Amen.**

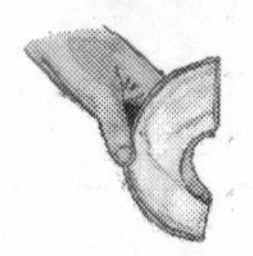

Faithfulness: The seventh fruit of the Holy Spirit

> **But the fruit of the Spirit is love, joy, peace, patience, kindness, goodness, faithfulness, gentleness, and self-control. Against such things there is no Law. And those who belong to Christ Jesus have crucified the flesh with its passions and desires. If we live by the Spirit, let us also keep in step with the Spirit (Galatians 5:22-25).**

***Pistos*: faithful, reliable, trustworthy, believing.**

Biblically, a faithful person is one who has become convinced that Jesus is the Messiah and the author of salvation.

There are many uses of *pistos*, the Greek word for faith and faithfulness. God is faithful and keeps His promises; people are 'the faithful'—those who believe in God and Jesus Christ, those who believe in the scriptures, and those who are loyal to the Faith.

We seek to be faithful in all that God has asked of us, and we trust in His faithfulness and believe the truth of His word.

> **Now faith is the assurance of things hoped for, the conviction of things not seen (Hebrew 11:1).**

The God of Faithfulness

> **Know therefore that the Lord your God is God, the faithful God who keeps covenant and steadfast love with those who love him and keep his commandments, to a thousand generations (Deuteronomy 7:9).**

The Bible is full of God's faithfulness. He is the Almighty, the creator of the world. He is omnipotent. There is no reason for God being unfaithful or forgetting His promises. We have the assurance that He will never change or go back on His word. He is the same yesterday, today, and forever.

How wonderful to have a Father like ours—we who are faithless, sinful, and ever-changing. We, who are imperfect, and fail constantly. We, who give in to temptation, and are arrogant. We have the God of Faithfulness who keeps us in His hands through all of life's challenges.

God is perfect, never fails, is never tempted and is not arrogant. He is faithful, He is goodness, and He loves us. How can we not love Him in return?

If we trust God and are faithful, He will take our weaknesses and make us strong. In our fear, He can make us brave. In our confusion, He gives us clarity. It is only our lack of trust that brings the world's difficulties crashing around us. God has promised to care for the faithful, and He keeps His promises.

He knows what troubles us and how often we are tempted to give in to our earthly desires. Who are we that God would want to commune with us, that He would send His son to die in our place to save us from eternal death? We are His children.

> **But the Lord is faithful. He will establish you and guard you against the evil one (2 Thessalonians 3:3).**

When we come before God and humbly ask for His forgiveness and help, He helps us. A thousand generations of people all over the world are in His loving care, and yet, He listens to our needs.

We see the evil in the world, the homeless, the hurting, and the vicious. Satan brought these evils, and the world accepted them as truth. The world embraced them. However, some of us heard God knocking at our door, and our spirits jumped for joy. He had faithfully waited for us to come to Him.

Now we are His children, and He will never leave us. The evil of the world is still around us, but because we have chosen to follow Christ instead of Satan, God will work in our lives to guide us into whom He wants us to be and on the path that He wants us to follow.

> **God is not man, that he should lie, or a son of man, that he should change his mind. Has he said, and will he not do it? Or has he spoken, and will he not fulfill it? (Numbers 23:19).**

This great faithfulness and love of our Father are difficult to understand because we are human, we lie, and we change our minds. We are unfaithful to the one who gave us life. To have someone utterly reliable and perfect on our side should make trust and faith in Him easy, but it is unnatural for us.

> **For the word of the Lord is upright, and all his work is done in faithfulness (Psalm 33:4).**

However, even when we continue to question and doubt, He loves us and continues to work all things for our good. He only asks that we love Him and are faithful to His word.

When we find comfort for every problem, every issue, and every frustration examined and explained in the Bible, we have confirmation that He is faithful and understands what we are going through.

> **But you, O Lord, are a God merciful and gracious, slow to anger and abounding in steadfast love and faithfulness (Psalm 86:15).**

Our own faithfulness pales in comparison. May we grow ever more faithful by reading His word and holding fast to the hope of our salvation.

> **Let us hold fast the confession of our hope without wavering, for he who promised is faithful (Hebrews 10:23).**

Prayer: **Father, forgive our weaknesses. Make us stronger, wiser and more faithful in all our ways to you. Our troubles in the world are nothing in the face of such a great and loving God. Thank you for your comfort. Thank you for your faithfulness. We want to bring to you so much more than what we have. Our brokenness is not worthy, but you are merciful. We praise you, Lord. Amen.**

Christ, the Only Way to Salvation

And the Lord God commanded the man, saying, "You may surely eat of every tree of the garden, but of the tree of the knowledge of good and evil you shall not eat, for in the day that you eat of it you shall surely die." (Genesis 2:16-17).

Adam and Eve failed in their relationship with God. They were not faithful to God's instructions and strayed from the truth.

God created a place for them to have a perfect relationship with Him. He gave them free will because he wanted them to love Him for who He was, not for what He did for them. He told them that if they ate from the tree of good and evil, they would die (not die instantly but bring death and the decay of their bodies over time).

When this happened, our perfect relationship with God broke. Adam and Eve sinned. God cannot look upon sin because He is perfect, but God had a plan to restore our relationship with Him. Through Christ, we have a second chance to live the life God wants for us and to commune with Him.

"For God so loved the world, that he gave his only Son, that whoever believes in him should not perish but have eternal life. For God did not send his Son into the world to condemn the world, but in order that the world might be saved through him. Whoever believes in him is not condemned, but whoever does not believe is condemned already, because he has not believed in the name of the only Son of God" (John 3:16-18).

God's plan, until the time of Jesus, took a while through wars and unfaithful people who did not do what God asked of them. When God sent His only son, born of a virgin, to be crucified for our sins and to rise again on the third day, the plan to bring us back into right relationship with Him was complete. As Jesus said on the cross, "It is finished."

We must accept this great gift. Accepting that Christ died in our place is the only way to have a right relationship with God. Confessing that He died for our sins will change our lives. Jesus Christ is the only way to have eternal life with God. In Him we are alive.

> **For as in Adam all die, so also in Christ shall all be made alive (1 Corinthians 15:22).**

This was all foretold in the Old Testament writings. Jesus Christ's life and crucifixion fulfilled every prophecy.

> **For by grace you have been saved through faith. And this is not your own doing; it is the gift of God, not a result of works, so that no one may boast (Ephesians 2:8-9).**

Everyone is searching for something in this life that will give them a sense of fulfillment. The world is falling apart. People are searching for anything that will make them happy, but happiness is fleeting. The joy of the Lord is eternal.

It is up to us to reach out to this lost and dying world, showing them the difference between happiness and joy, the difference between Christianity and worldliness. We are the ones who are able to tell the world that Christ is the only way to salvation.

> **Because, if you confess with your mouth that Jesus is Lord and believe in your heart that God raised him from the dead, you will be saved (Romans 10:9).**

> *Prayer:* **Lord, let our lives always show the love of your son Jesus Christ. We want to be faithful in all things, including showing your love to those around us. The world needs you, and they will only know you if we show and tell them why you are the only way to salvation. Amen.**

Making Time for God

But seek first his kingdom and his righteousness, and all these things will be given to you as well (Matthew 6:33).

Time is a precious commodity these days. We get up in the morning, and the rat race begins. Many of us start with coffee, then the kids, shower, and dress. Then we are off to work.

We check our Facebook and email, finish that great book we were reading, watch TV, plan our vacation, pay bills, study, go to class, take care of the kids/pets/parents/spouse, go grocery shopping, do the dishes, wash clothes, clean house, get gas, do yard work... day after day.

Don't worry, we tell ourselves; we can go to church on Sunday, and that is enough to take care of the God part. Of course, lots of Christians feel that Sunday is the only opportunity available to spend time with their family, so even church attendance is sparse.

Church is a great place to spend an hour or two with your family. We pray for blessings, yet we often begrudge a little of our time to God. We need to be faithful to our Lord, who has richly blessed us. We need to make time for God if we are going to ask Him to make time for us.

We are very good at making excuses to God about why we can't spend time with Him. We don't have time to read a verse in the Bible daily because we need our sleep. We don't have time to start each day or end each day in prayer or to talk to God constantly because we have so much on our minds. "We are stressed, we are busy, we are late, but we still want your blessings, Lord."

There is only one real reason we do not give time to God. It is because the devil doesn't want us to. We are not being faithful and making time for God because Satan wants to hold us back from developing a strong relationship with God and receiving all the blessings and gifts God has for those who love Him. The devil is winning this battle, and we are allowing it.

Be alert and of sober mind. Your enemy the devil prowls around like a roaring lion looking for someone to devour (1 Peter 5:8).

Yes, there is one God, and yes, there is a devil (fallen angel). There is good, and there is evil, and the evil wants to keep us so busy that the good is stolen from us. This is a battle for our time.

Of the approximately 900 minutes a day that we are awake, we can spend a few of those talking to God, asking for His fruit, and reading His word. We are able to listen to His word being read aloud to us on our phones, computers, Alexa, Siri, or Google. Staying in God's word is easier than it has ever been with today's technology. We have no excuse.

The things the world requires of us in this life are the very reasons faithfulness to God is important. We can't let another day go by without giving time to Him. He deserves it, and we need it. It's simple.

> **When you vow a vow to God, do not delay paying it, for he has no pleasure in fools. Pay what you vow. It is better that you should not vow than that you should vow and not pay. Let not your mouth lead you into sin, and do not say before the messenger that it was a mistake. Why should God be angry at your voice and destroy the work of your hands? For when dreams increase and words grow many, there is vanity; but God is the one you must fear (Ecclesiastes 5:4-7).**

We vowed to follow Christ, love and serve Him. Now we are gradually neglecting to pay our vow. When our dreams increase and words grow many, there is vanity, as in Ecclesiastes.

We dream of bigger houses, better jobs, and more things and we spend much time talking about and seeking those things. We don't fear (respect) God as we ought.

God is not mocked. Would we have a relationship with people who won't talk to us or spend time with us? We owe God what we vowed, being faithful as He is faithful.

> **Look carefully then how you walk, not as unwise but as wise, making the best use of the time, because the days are evil. Therefore, do not be foolish, but understand what the will of the Lord is (Ecclesiastes 5:15-17).**

As we walk through this day, let us walk with the Lord. Our time is precious, and so is His. His will is for our good, and He will make sure we have time for the other things we think are so important.

But I trust in you, O Lord; I say, "You are my God." My times are in your hand; rescue me from the hand of my enemies and from my persecutors! (Psalms 31:14-15).

Prayer: **Lord, let our time be in your hands. Let us give our time to you, talking to you, walking with you and being faithful as you are faithful. Protect our minds from running away to other things. We love you and trust you and give ourselves to you this day and always. Amen.**

Social Media is Not the Bible

> **"Finally, brothers and sisters, whatever is true, whatever is noble, whatever is right, whatever is pure, whatever is lovely, whatever is admirable — if anything is excellent or praiseworthy — think about such things and the God of peace will be with you" (Philippians 4:8).**

Social media is a wonderful tool for sharing family photos, events, reconnecting with old friends and so much more. Unfortunately, as we all know, sometimes things show up that we really don't want to see and can't un-see.

Social media posts are often the opposite of what the Apostle Paul wanted us to think about. As faithful followers of Christ, this should concern us. Social media is not the Bible.

Sometimes we see posts that at first glance seem positive and scriptural, but after reflection, we realize that they are not. There are many seemingly positive web pages and positive affirmations of which we should be careful. God's way is different and often misunderstood.

When you read a post that says, "what you allow is what will continue," what do you think? On the surface, this may seem true. Why should we allow negative things in our lives to continue? We need to get it out, stop it, or throw a fit...but what about from Christ's view? What would Jesus say about this?

> **But love your enemies, and do good, and lend, expecting nothing in return, and your reward will be great, and you will be sons of the Most High, for he is kind to the ungrateful and the evil (Luke 6:35).**

We can see that, although the post seems logical, it is not a true statement from God's perspective. When reading social media posts and supposed affirmations of faith, we need to be wise and consider what the Bible has to say. If something sounds right but is not faithful to God's word, then it is a lie.

> **"Now, Lord God, let your promise to my father David be confirmed, for you have made me king over a people who**

are as numerous as the dust of the earth. *Give me wisdom and knowledge*, that I may lead this people, for who is able to govern this great people of yours?" (2 Chronicles 1:9-10).

We must pray for wisdom and knowledge—knowledge so that we understand the true meaning of what we read and see, and wisdom to know how to handle that knowledge. Perhaps we should just ignore the messages. Perhaps God may lead us to explain, to the person who wrote it, why it is not of Him.

I appeal to you, brothers, to watch out for those who cause divisions and create obstacles contrary to the doctrine that you have been taught; avoid them (Romans 16:17).

The Bible has wisdom on every subject. We can find answers to every question in God's word. When we read and see things on social media that are divisive or cause us to question Christian teachings, we need to take time to pray and to discern whether it agrees with God's word.

For the time is coming when people will not endure sound teaching, but having itching ears they will accumulate for themselves teachers to suit their own passions (2 Timothy 4:3).

The world today is looking for the easy way to everything. Even God's faithful want immediate satisfaction. We want anything and everything that makes us feel good, especially about ourselves. Social media is a perfect tool for the devil to use to confuse us and make things that draw us away from being faithful to God sound good.

God knew that these days were coming. He knew about social media before humans invented it. We are not the ones who should have itching ears, reading and listening only to words that make us comfortable and feel good. We are faithful to God's teaching and apply it to our lives.

See to it that no one takes you captive by philosophy and empty deceit, according to human tradition, according to the elemental spirits of the world, and not according to Christ (Colossians 2:8).

Emails and posts that say we must pass something on to receive a blessing from God are not true. That is not how God works. Just because we read something on social media does not make it so. The Bible is the word of God and will never contradict itself.

Now is the time for our righteous anger. The world is being fooled and Christians along with them. Christ died for our sins. He rose again and sent His Holy Spirit to teach us and help us to get wisdom. We need to stand on God's words, not the words on social media.

> **Now the Spirit expressly says that in later times some will depart from the faith by devoting themselves to deceitful spirits and teachings of demons, through the insincerity of liars whose consciences are seared (1 Timothy 4:1).**

It should amaze and comfort us that the Bible predicts everything that is happening now and forevermore.

There is more going on in this world than we will ever know. The spiritual battle that is happening all around us is a fight for our very souls. If social media is negatively affecting our relationship with God, we need to leave it behind, as we would anything else that causes unfaithfulness.

Stay in prayer and read the real Bible. These are the ways to protect ourselves and others from the war that is being waged. Pray for those who spend all their time on social media, that they will be faithful to God and be wise in their use of these tools.

> ***Prayer:*** **Lord, technology is everywhere. Make us wise users of these tools, using them to shine your light into this world. Make us faithful in all things for your glory. Lead us away from the temptations that they may pose. Help us to see the wolf in sheep's clothing and be guided by your Holy Spirit. Amen.**

Life is Eternal

And [the wicked] will go away into eternal punishment, but the righteous into eternal life (Matthew 25:46).

We think of eternal life as a positive thing. Preachers talk about accepting that Jesus died for our sins, forgiveness and receiving eternal life, and that is true. What we don't hear is that all life is eternal, and some will not spend eternity with God.

When our earthly bodies die, our souls live on. Heaven is our way of saying eternity with God, where there is no pain, no anger, and no evil. That is why we must come to Him through the blood that Jesus sacrificed for our sins. Jesus makes us clean and pure by His blood. That is the only way we will live with God for eternity.

Heaven might be another dimension that we are not aware of, or it might be an actual, physical place. We do know that the Bible tells us that there is no pain or suffering there. We know that we can only spend our eternity there if we are washed by the blood of Jesus.

If all life is eternal, then there is another place opposite of eternity with God, and that is eternity *without* God. If there is no pain or suffering in heaven, then there must be pain and suffering in Hell.

We can't believe in eternity with God and not believe that the opposite is also true or that death without knowing God is just nothingness. The Bible tells us differently.

There is an opposite to everything. The Bible speaks about good and evil, truth and lies, light and darkness, wisdom and foolishness, knowledge and ignorance, remembering and forgetting, innocence and guilt, beginning and end, beauty and ugliness, design and chance, heaven and hell, and finally, God and Satan. You can't have one without the other.

Hellfire and brimstone aren't preached much these days for fear someone might be offended. Hell is a complicated subject and may seem cruel, but we all have the opportunity to spend eternity with God. Everyone has free will to accept His gift of life with Him.

For God so loved the world, that he gave his only Son, that whoever believes in him should not perish but have eternal life (John 3:16).

Hell may also be another dimension or an actual place. What we know is that it is not with God, that God cannot look upon sin and that there will be suffering because it is the opposite of eternal life with God.

The Bible language used was very specific for that age and culture to understand what eternal death will be. Whether the fire is fire as we know it or was a metaphor, we do not know, and it doesn't matter. What matters is that we don't spend our eternity there.

> **For the wages of sin is death, but the free gift of God is eternal life in Christ Jesus our Lord (Romans 6:23).**

Not making a choice to follow Christ is a choice. So not making a choice to spend eternity with God is making a choice to spend eternity apart from Him. We need to make a choice, and we need the world around us to know that they have a choice, too.

> **And if anyone's name was not found written in the book of life, he was thrown into the lake of fire (Revelation 20:15).**

> ***Prayer:* Lord, please reach out to our loved ones who have not chosen you. Please do not let them die in their sins. Let us be faithful in all things so that we can show others the truth about you. Give us words when needed to explain your great gift of Jesus. Amen.**

Why Should We Attend Church?

Praise the Lord! Praise God in his sanctuary; praise him in his mighty heavens! Praise him for his mighty deeds; praise him according to his excellent greatness! Praise him with trumpet sound; praise him with lute and harp! Praise him with tambourine and dance; praise him with strings and pipe! Praise him with sounding cymbals; praise him with loud clashing cymbals! (Psalm 150:1-6).

There is very little good news in the world today. We become worn down by the negative stories we see and read about. We see news of fighting, death, storms, stealing, lying, cheating, hatred and evil. We look forward to Friday and hope for a peaceful weekend.

This is the world in which we live. It is scary and speeding by, running us over without regard. But God is faithful. We can rely on His promises to care for us. He promises He is with us through all of it.

As Christians, we need the refreshing that comes from God and from each other. We need people who believe as we do and who will encourage and uplift us in troubling times. Our homes are where we can rest and be ourselves, and that is a place of peace. It is the same with God's home, the house of God, the church.

Here there is not Greek and Jew, circumcised and uncircumcised, barbarian, Scythian, slave, free; but Christ is all, and in all (Colossians 3:11).

Attending church takes time, and certainly, we can worship anywhere and anytime. Yes, there are some who are hypocritical in the church, but these are excuses for not being faithful to God. If we were to find a perfect church, it wouldn't be perfect once we joined. The devil is working overtime in this world, and we are not even putting in our 40 hours for God. We should be able to give Him at least one hour a week.

Praise the Lord! I will give thanks to the Lord with my whole heart, in the company of the upright, in the congregation (Psalm 111:1).

We need to attend church and be in the company of the upright. We don't have to worry about minor things like being late or what we are wearing. It doesn't matter if we know the songs. Just being with God's people brings needed refreshing and peace.

> **And let us consider how to stir up one another to love and good works, not neglecting to meet together, as is the habit of some, but encouraging one another, and all the more as you see the Day drawing near (Hebrews 10:24-25).**

One or two hours a week is not too much to give to God. Our children need Sunday school, and we need to worship, sing and praise God for all His faithfulness. The church is a place to find peace, to renew our minds, to calm down and breathe, to give our fears to God, and to be taught so that we may grow stronger. We must become stronger as our world becomes more evil and belief in God becomes unpopular.

> **Do not be conformed to this world, but be transformed by the renewal of your mind, that by testing you may discern what is the will of God, what is good and acceptable and perfect (Romans 12:2).**

Not attending church will cause us to slip away from a close relationship with God. The longer we allow ourselves to go without attending, the easier it becomes, and the less time we will spend with God daily. Eventually, the world closes in around us, and we try to serve two masters, the world and God.

> **No one can serve two masters, for either he will hate the one and love the other, or he will be devoted to the one and despise the other (Matthew 6:24).**

Other Christians are our family. How wonderful to know that we all worship our Father, love each other, and are obedient to His word. We are free to be in church, a safe, loving place, being renewed for the coming week. God is so happy when we faithfully worship Him together.

> **But you are a chosen race, a royal priesthood, a holy na-**

tion, a people for his own possession, that you may proclaim the excellencies of him who called you out of darkness into his marvelous light (1 Peter 2:9).

Prayer: **Lord, gathering together to worship you is so very valuable to us. Help us understand that you deserve our time and our gratitude and that from you we receive mercy and grace. We need to let you know how much we love you and how grateful we are for your gifts and for watching over us. Let us bow our knees at your greatness with others who are faithful. You are Lord. Amen.**

The Supernatural and the Christian

Now the (Holy) Spirit expressly says that in later times some will depart from the faith by devoting themselves to deceitful spirits and teachings of demons (1 Timothy 4:1).

Discussions about the supernatural are common these days. There are television shows about ghosts and supernatural events. Some call themselves psychics, tarot card readers, magicians, people who talk to or see the dead. These things are an abomination to the Lord. And yet, fascination with them grows. We are blind to the truth of these practices. They are evil, and they will take our minds from the truth and simplicity of God's salvation through Christ.

...anyone who practices divination or tells fortunes or interprets omens, or a sorcerer or a charmer or a medium or a necromancer or one who inquires of the dead, for whoever does these things is an abomination to the Lord (Deuteronomy 18:9-13).

It is possible that some people experience 'supernatural' things. But—**and this is very important**—these spirits are not whom we think they are. These are tricks of the devil to draw attention away from the true spirit of the Holy God. Allowing these enticements to draw us away will mean eternal death.

Do not turn to mediums or necromancers; do not seek them out, and so make yourselves unclean by them: I am the Lord your God (Leviticus 19:31).

When people get involved with and start believing in what is not of God, but is still called supernatural, they are worshiping and believing in idols and things that God's word tells us are evil. They are not taking their concerns to God. They are relying on unknown spirits to help them. They are trusting in other sources.

God's way is often unseen, but these supernatural things are visible because Satan wants them visible and are seemingly real, so easy to see and hear. We like things that we can see and hear. It makes us comfortable, and the devil knows it. Having faith in what we can't see is much harder.

And when they say to you, "Inquire of the mediums and the necromancers who chirp and mutter," should not a people inquire of their God? Should they inquire of the dead on behalf of the living? (Isaiah 8:19).

God's way is so simple, but it seems we want things complicated. Being involved in something strange and dangerous interests us. Salvation is almost too simple. We want amazement. We are a strange people. God's way is so much more amazing but takes faith!

For such men are false apostles, deceitful workmen, disguising themselves as apostles of Christ. And no wonder, for even Satan disguises himself as an angel of light. So it is no surprise if his servants, also, disguise themselves as servants of righteousness. Their end will correspond to their deeds (2 Corinthians 11:13-15).

Even if these spirits profess to be of God and speak about Him as though He was their God, they are lying. We must be wary of the false spirits, false prophets, and false gods.

For we do not wrestle against flesh and blood, but against the rulers, against the authorities, against the cosmic powers over this present darkness, against the spiritual forces of evil in the heavenly places (Ephesians 6:12).

We might ask ourselves, "What about God's angels watching out for us?" God's angels spoke to the prophets, appeared to Mary and Joseph, watched out for Christ, appeared when He rose from the dead, and have popped up a few times in the Bible mostly speaking to the prophets before Christ came.

Angels may surround us and minister to us; we don't know. We do know that they will never detract from or contradict the word of God or Christ and His crucifixion. They are not equal to Christ. They are not our focus and are not worshiped or prayed to. If we are faithful to God, we do not need to dwell on how He is going to work in our lives. We can just be thankful.

Long ago, at many times and in many ways, God spoke to our fathers by the prophets, [2] but in these last days he has spoken to us by his Son (Hebrews 1:1,2).

Some Christians like to study the supernatural, and they move further and further away from God's simple salvation. It would be better to study the life of Christ, His crucifixion, rising from the dead, being seen by the disciples, and ascending into heaven. This is fascinating enough.

The intense interest in this issue is becoming so prevalent that we need to take it very seriously and avoid all contact. It may seem silly, but we should refrain from cartoons, movies, TV shows, fiction, nonfiction, songs, concerts, or anything that promotes this subject.

We may know it is false and tell ourselves that we just enjoy watching or listening, but what we put into our minds stays there and is dwelt (or meditated) on. It makes an impact on us. We want to dwell on God alone.

Let the words of my mouth and the <u>meditation</u> of my heart be acceptable in your sight, O Lord, my rock and my redeemer (Psalm 19:14).

Be faithful to God alone and speak only to Him. We cannot speak with our departed loved ones. The ghosts that people may see or think they see are workers of the devil. The shows we watch are promoted by and promote the powers of darkness. It is all a lie. Christ is the only truth.

Jesus said to him, "I am the way, and the truth, and the life. No one comes to the Father except through me" (John 14:6).

***Prayer:* Almighty Father, we worship you alone. Do not allow us to be drawn away by the false teachers or spiritual evils that are everywhere we look. We pledge to be faithful to you alone, your word and your teachings. Thank you for your protection. Amen.**

Standing Strong

Be strong and courageous. Do not fear or be in dread of them, for it is the Lord your God who goes with you. He will not leave you or forsake you (Deuteronomy 31:6).

We all have ups and downs in life. Sometimes things go along somewhat smoothly and then *crash*—something happens that feels like the bottom just fell out, and our faith in God wavers.

Many are fighting addictions, have health problems, have lost loved ones, are looking for jobs, or are having family issues. We all suffer from things that bring us to our knees. We make choices. We try to stand strong when it feels like everything is falling apart, or we allow the pain to overtake us.

It would be nice if we could just have faith and a 'no problem, everything will work out' attitude, but we have difficulty trusting God every moment. We are human. We have different reactions to difficulties, and that is the way God made us. He uses these situations to build our faith and trust in Him.

Each of us reacts differently when something bad happens. Some of us react initially by crying, worrying and fretting, but then our faith strengthens, and we handle it more calmly.

Some react calmly at first, telling others it will all be okay and then later become scared and worried, losing a measure of faith.

How we react at first is okay. We have not failed God if we don't have it all together immediately when bad things happen or if our faith wavers later. We just need to remember to take these trials before the Lord.

Every issue or trouble that we face is in the Bible. We can draw faith from the scriptures as we research our situation. That's why the word of God is here for us, and admittedly in the past, the Bible could be hard to read and understand. We have no excuse today. We can Google what the Bible says about any topic and find the scriptures almost instantaneously.

For we walk by faith, not by sight (2 Corinthians 5:7).

When life hits us hard, we need to wait on God and walk by faith.

Taking time to pray, expressing our love for Him, and bringing the troubling events before Him will give us peace. Reading what the word of God has to say about it will calm us.

Every day His strength will carry us, and whatever caused us grief will pass. We can have confidence that God is working in the situation for our good. We can stand strong.

In difficult situations, God wants us to have faith in Him, trusting that He has a plan, doing what we know is right, and leaving the rest to Him. Some say that belief in God is a crutch. Crutches help people stand, so we are happy to have that crutch to help us stand when nonbelievers fall.

> **"I have said these things to you, that in me you may have peace. In the world you will have tribulation. But take heart; I have overcome the world" (John 16:33).**

There are times when all we can do is pray "Thy will be done." God understands the pain and the inability to put into words what we are feeling. We call upon the name of Jesus and stand strong in our faith.

> **For we do not wrestle against flesh and blood, but against the rulers, against the authorities, against the cosmic powers over this present darkness, against the spiritual forces of evil in the heavenly places (Ephesians 6:12).**

We may think that our problems are earth-born. In other words, we think that they come from people, places or things here on earth. But we know we are in a war against the powers of darkness. Our problems and our battles come from the evil one, who is trying to break our faith.

God's Holy Spirit will instruct and encourage us. These troubles will pass. Have faith, stand strong. He has overcome the world.

> ***Prayer*: Heavenly Father, strengthen our faith and let your Holy Spirit surround us as we face challenges in our lives. We know that you are with us and together we are fighting a battle against the evils of this world. Help us to stand strong in our faith, never wavering, holding fast to your promises, with peace in our hearts. Amen.**

Gentleness: The eighth fruit of the Holy Spirit

But the fruit of the Spirit is love, joy, peace, patience, kindness, goodness, faithfulness, gentleness, and self-control. Against such things there is no Law. And those who belong to Christ Jesus have crucified the flesh with its passions and desires. If we live by the Spirit, let us also keep in step with the Spirit (Galatians 5:22-25).

> ***Praýtēs – meekness* ('gentle strength') which expresses *power*** with ***reserve and gentleness*** (Strong's Concordance).

For Christians, the word *gentleness* means using a powerful, gentle strength inspired by God to show God's love to the world. This gentleness only comes through faith in God and His son Jesus Christ and allows us to react to life in this world, not as doormats, but as bright lights to the world.

It is also used to show God's gentleness to us as we follow Him while we deal with a maze of evil.

So flee youthful passions and pursue righteousness, faith, love, and peace, along with those who call on the Lord from a pure heart. Have nothing to do with foolish, ignorant controversies; you know that they breed quarrels. And the Lord's servant must not be quarrelsome but kind to everyone, able to teach, patiently enduring evil, correcting his opponents with gentleness. God may perhaps grant them repentance leading to a knowledge of the truth (2 Timothy 2:22-25).

The God of Gentleness

To speak evil of no one, to avoid quarreling, to be gentle, and to show perfect courtesy toward all people (Titus 3:2).

Even for the most mature Christian, showing perfect courtesy to all people is asking a lot. Thankfully, God has no difficulty with this and is willing to give this fruit to us.

We know God is powerful, but did we know that His gentleness also has power? He guides us gently, and our gentleness requires a certain control in our hands if it is used properly. Without control, gentleness is not gentle; it is lax and weak.

Think of the gentle way we hold a baby. If we do not control our gentleness with strength, the baby will fall. In all the Bible's gentleness, this strength is necessary. We cannot confuse the gentleness of God with being weak, and we cannot confuse being gentle with others as a weakness in ourselves.

You have given me the shield of your salvation, and your right hand supported me, and your gentleness made me great (Psalm 18:35).

God's gentleness makes us great. We are not weak. We are the army of God. May we not forget gentleness in our dealings, or else we may react as the world reacts or become so busy that gentleness is not on our minds.

There are church programs to run, worship services to practice, Sunday School classes to teach. We are ready to make our opinions known in all things and forget about the God of gentleness.

It is easy to quarrel and disagree. We have our own opinions, and we may believe we have the right to express them however they come out of our mouths. We want to defend our ideas and change the minds of those who disagree. We are decidedly un-gentle.

But the Lord tells us specifically to avoid quarreling, to be gentle, and to show perfect courtesy toward all people. Rarely can we express a strong contrary opinion and avoid quarreling unless we have the fruit of gentleness.

Power, reserve, respect, and gentleness are all part of gentleness and are all attributes of our great God. He will instill this in us if we ask Him and as we mature in our relationship with Christ. God is patient with us as we strive to become more like Jesus, and He is always gentle with us.

> **But in your hearts honor Christ the Lord as holy, always being prepared to make a defense to anyone who asks you for a reason for the hope that is in you; yet do it with gentleness and respect (1 Peter 3:15).**

If we use the gentle strength of God, we can discuss without argument and express our opinions without fear or anger. If we feel the gentleness of God in us, we may decide that our opinions are not worth expressing anyway. Many quarrels and disagreements are vain and worthless.

There is only one position we need to be ready to defend, and that is our belief in Jesus Christ. If we are gentle, we may lead a lost one to salvation, and that is what really matters in this world.

> **And the Lord's servant must not be quarrelsome but kind to everyone, able to teach, patiently enduring evil, correcting his opponents with gentleness. God may perhaps grant them repentance leading to a knowledge of the truth (2 Timothy 2:24-25).**

> ***Prayer:*** **Lord, you are gentle, and you are strong. When we are called to be strong, let us also be gentle. Do not allow quarreling and strife to be caused by us, in the body of Christ, or wherever we are. We want to show your love to each other and to the world. Amen.**

Defending the Faith

But in your hearts honor Christ the Lord as holy, always being prepared to make a defense to anyone who asks you for a reason for the hope that is in you; yet do it with gentleness and respect (1 Peter 3:15).

The only thing we need to defend is Christ. Nothing else is important enough to spend our breath to defend. Truly, if we think of all the issues we feel strongly about, whether it is politics, health food, animal rights, the right to bear arms, financial matters, or the like, chances are we will not change the view of the people we are quarreling with no matter how long we argue. Christ doesn't want us quarreling about those things anyway.

When it comes to defending the reason that we live and believe as we do, though, Our Holy Savior, who died for our sins, will prepare us through His word. Even still, the Lord requires that we defend Him with His gentleness and respect.

Often, we see groups of people defending Christianity in a strong way but miss the gentle part. Perhaps some of us have even joined in protests or arguments that got heated and angry. This is not what God has instructed us. And, of course, there have been wars fought over religious beliefs, including Christianity.

You have given me the shield of your salvation, and your right hand supported me, and your gentleness made me great (Psalm 18:35).

Using God's gentleness makes us great, as in the Psalm, in our conversation. If we want to do as the Lord has instructed us, we become ready to defend our faith, while avoiding conflict over other unimportant and worldly issues. Minds are rarely changed when quarreling, even when presented with facts.

There have been many studies about why minds in quarrels do not change. One of the reasons is our wish to win the argument. Even when presented with facts, our minds are not reasonable. On social media, where we see many arguments, according to a Facebook study, only 20 percent of people ever change their minds on an issue. That is with quarreling, but what about gentleness?

There is only one topic worth defending, and yet, it is the one topic we sometimes avoid at all costs. We are uncomfortable sharing Christianity. We are unwilling or not ready to share. We fear being scoffed at or not being knowledgeable to make a strong stand for Christ. We fear an argument will break out.

> **And the Lord's servant must not be quarrelsome but kind to everyone, able to teach, patiently enduring evil, correcting his opponents with gentleness. God may perhaps grant them repentance leading to a knowledge of the truth, and they may come to their senses and escape from the snare of the devil, after being captured by him to do his will (2 Timothy 2:24-26).**

Defending our faith does not require scholars of the Bible or great orators. It is easiest to gently tell our own story and how God has changed us. Others find it impossible to challenge us over our own true events.

Talking about our lives before we asked Christ into our hearts, and our lives after, can have a profound effect. People like stories and are searching for something to give their lives greater meaning. God is the only one who can, so when we tell our story with gentleness, they may listen. Pushy people are rarely listened to.

> **A soft answer turns away wrath, but a harsh word stirs up anger (Proverbs 15:1).**

There is never a time when a Christian should get into a shouting match with a nonbeliever. Even if they hurt our feelings, even if they are completely wrong in their interpretation of events in the Bible, even if they do not know the difference between the Old and New Testaments and the Old and New Covenants, we cannot call them names or berate them for their unbelief. Even if they don't believe that Jesus is the son of God or that there is a God, we must be gentle and respectful.

The same God we are telling them about is working in their lives, though they probably don't know it. He loves them just as He loves us, and it is His plan to bring them into a relationship with Him. He will never give up on them, and He will never be angry with them. He will always be gentle.

We can follow His example by continuing to tell them what has happened in our own lives and showing how much we trust God in the rough times.

Deep Biblical questions may throw us, but "This is what I know" is a good way to answer their questions, followed by our own personal experiences. Then we can pray for these people. Prayer is powerful, and God hears.

The will of the Father for His children is to be wise, avoiding quarrels about things that don't matter to the kingdom and being ready to defend the truth of Jesus Christ with the gentleness from the Holy Spirit. If we ask for wisdom and gentleness, He will give them to us, full of mercy and good fruit.

But the wisdom from above is first pure, then peaceable, gentle, open to reason, full of mercy and good fruits, impartial and sincere (James 3:17).

Prayer: **Father, thank you for sending your son to save us. Help us know how and when to share the good news with those around us. Give us boldness when defending our faith with gentleness and love. Amen.**

The Lord is My Shepherd

A Psalm of David (Psalm 23).

The Lord is my shepherd; I shall not want.
He makes me lie down in green pastures.
He leads me beside still waters.
He restores my soul.
He leads me in paths of righteousness
for his name's sake.

Even though I walk through the valley of the shadow of death,
I will fear no evil,
for you are with me;
your rod and your staff, they comfort me.

You prepare a table before me
in the presence of my enemies;
you anoint my head with oil;
my cup overflows.
Surely goodness and mercy shall follow me
all the days of my life,
and I shall dwell in the house of the Lord
forever.

Many of us grew us memorizing the 23rd Psalm, and if we didn't, we have at least heard it during our lifetimes. The psalm encourages and lifts us up when we are going through rough patches. Taking time to think about this well-known Psalm is eye-opening and inspiring.

It begins by comparing us to sheep with our shepherd. Even though this psalm came many years before the birth of Christ, the Shepherd is Jesus, the son of God who gave His life for us.

Shepherds were known for taking great care of their sheep and for being gentle. They lived with them, slept with them and rescued them when they were in trouble. They even carried them on their shoulders. The shepherd took their flocks to the best areas for grazing and pure water. Their sheep felt safe.

Jesus does the same for us. He provides the best for those who love Him, and He restores not only our physical bodies, but our souls. If we love and follow Him, we will follow the path of righteousness, and when times are bad, we are not afraid, knowing that Jesus is always with us.

The rod and staff are compared to the word of God and His Spirit. They are gentle and comforting because they were used to guide, but the rod and staff were also strong and used to protect the sheep in times of danger, so even though we will experience evil, we are not afraid.

King David went on to describe how the Lord honored Him in front of His enemies and God anointed his head with oil. Oil had many uses. It was used to anoint one as King. It was also used to set someone apart as holy for God's use. Oil was also used to anoint for healing.

When God anoints a head with oil, we know it is a great honor, and that person is well loved, protected, provided for, and guided by Him. His cup surely overflowed. We are not royalty, but Christ gave His life for us and anointed us with His blood.

Because of all that God had done for King David, he knew that if He followed the path that God laid out for Him, the goodness of God would follow Him along with mercy for His mistakes. After his life on earth, he would be with God in heaven.

What a great psalm for us today. He is our shepherd. If we love and follow Him, He will gently guide us, love us, provide for us, protect us, and set us apart for His use. We will live with Him for eternity.

The Lord is my shepherd, I shall not want.

> ***Prayer:*** **Father, thank you for being our Shepherd through this life that is truly difficult. Thank you for your guidance and the great mercy that you give to each of us. You are our gentle shepherd, and we know that we are never alone, for you are always with us. Amen.**

Leave the Past in the Past

Not that I have already obtained this or am already perfect, but I press on to make it my own, because Christ Jesus has made me his own. Brothers, I do not consider that I have made it my own. But one thing I do: forgetting what lies behind and straining forward to what lies ahead, I press on toward the goal for the prize of the upward call of God in Christ Jesus (Philippians 3:12-14).

We all have a past. We all have things we wish we hadn't done. We cannot go back and change the past, so we must strive not to live there in our hearts and minds. God wants us to move on and to move forward with Him.

Our pasts, in part, made us who we are. When we accepted Christ into our hearts, we were made new creations as if we were born again. We should now be moving forward in our relationship with God, not living in the mistakes of the past.

If we don't like who we are, even after becoming a believer, then our relationship with God is out of whack. We won't be able to rejoice until we draw closer to God and become whom He wants us to be. Sometimes, that involves being gentle with ourselves and taking the heavy chain of the past from around our necks and throwing it away.

Therefore, if anyone is in Christ, he is a new creation. The old has passed away; behold, the new has come (2 Corinthians 5:17).

There will still be times, even as Christians, when we do unchristian things. There will be times when we will know that what we are doing is wrong, or will regret something we said or did, and wish we could take it back. If we can make it right, we should, but otherwise, we need to ask God to forgive us and to help us so that it doesn't happen again.

We live in such a difficult world, surrounded by difficult, worldly people. It is overwhelming. However, God allows us to put our mistakes in the past along with the rest of our unholy actions. He forgives and gently leads us back as a shepherd guides his flock.

"I, I am he who blots out your transgressions for my own sake, and I will not remember your sin" (Isaiah 43:25).

Knowing we are forgiven is the only way we can get through life. If we keep running day after day while looking behind us, we will fall. If we keep doing the things that, to our minds, are important but are contrary to God's word, we will not succeed. We will do and say things we regret.

"Be still and know that I am God. I will be exalted among the nations, I will be exalted in the earth!" (Psalms 46:10).

If we take time to be still and realize that God will be exalted in the earth even though we have made mistakes, we can put our past behind us. We have confidence that God will take care of what needs doing. We feel refreshed and look ahead with a cheerful heart.

More than anyone else, we remember our own mistakes. We are our own worst critics. We punish ourselves repeatedly even after God has had mercy on us, forgiving us for our sins. Forgiving ourselves is much harder. We are gentle with others but not with ourselves.

When we find ourselves dwelling on past mistakes, sins, wrongdoings, and hurts, we must bring them to God for forgiveness and leave them at the foot of the cross. We are worthy through the blood of Christ. We are forgiven.

I have been crucified with Christ. It is no longer I who live, but Christ who lives in me. And the life I now live in the flesh I live by faith in the Son of God, who loved me and gave himself for me (Galatians 2:20).

Prayer: **Lord, we know that you have forgiven our sins, but we have difficulty forgetting what we have done. Please take away the shame that we feel and help us be gentle with ourselves, forgiving ourselves while we live our lives for you and your glory. Amen.**

What Can I Do for God?

Just as I try to please everyone in everything I do, not seeking my own advantage, but that of many, that they may be saved (1 Corinthians 10:33).

Our lives are all about work, bills, fun, family, and friends. We spend every day either working to support our lifestyle, spending time doing things, cleaning house, paying bills, going out, cooking, eating, taking care of family, and pets, etc.

This is how most people live. As Christians, we also worship God, attend church, ask Him to forgive us our shortcomings and to give us wisdom, strength, health, happiness, love, and whatever else we need and want. We need to slow down.

God, our heavenly father, loves us and understands, but He sent His only son to die and rise again so that we could have abundant life through Him. He is working to bring salvation to all. His wish is for everyone to accept Him, follow Him, and love Him. His plan has been in the works since Adam and Eve first sinned. Now He needs us to help bring it about, but we are too busy.

The Lord is not slow to fulfill his promise as some count slowness, but is patient toward you, not wishing that any should perish, but that all should reach repentance (2 Peter 3:9).

We know that God wants everyone to come to repentance. Repentance comes from hearing God's word and accepting His son. We need to help spread the word or at least show God's love to those around us. We should not be selfish with what God has given us.

Do not neglect to do good and to share what you have, for such sacrifices are pleasing to God (Hebrews 13:16).

Most of us would not be comfortable going out and witnessing on a street corner. If that is not what God has called us to do, then He has given us some other gift that will help to bring people into His kingdom.

We can pray for the lost, we can show love to the unloved. As

Christians filled with the love of God, we can give that love away and never run out. It takes nothing away from us to show another person kindness, to smile, to call them by name, to look them in the eye, or to tell them they look nice. We can thank them sincerely for just being there.

God is gentle with us, and we can be gentle in our dealings with others. Being dealt with harshly is not what anyone wants. Gentleness from the Holy Spirit is a great tool to show a very violent world the love of God.

No one wants to be made fun of or to feel out of place. We can help others feel comfortable and change someone's total outlook on life just by showing God's lovingkindness. When we show kindness, we honor the other person and let them know that they mean something in this world.

> **Therefore, my beloved brothers, be steadfast, immovable, always abounding in the work of the Lord, knowing that in the Lord your labor is not in vain (1 Corinthians 15:58).**

God may call us to do more practical work for Him. There are many ways to serve. There are many homeless people in need of donations or meals. We can befriend a new person in church, sit with them, and take them to lunch. We can teach a Sunday School class or volunteer in the nursery. We can invite our neighbors over for dinner. God will tell us what He wants us to do. We need to hear Him.

> **But be doers of the word, and not hearers only, deceiving yourselves (James 1:22).**

> ***Prayer:*** **God, help us make a difference in this messed up world. Each of us can make a difference to someone. What can we do for you today and every day? Help us to hear your voice and do what you want us to do. Take our selfishness from us and make us workers in your plan to bring salvation to all. Amen.**

Having a Christian Character

> **Put on then, as God's chosen ones, holy and beloved, compassionate hearts, kindness, humility, meekness, and patience, bearing with one another and, if one has a complaint against another, forgiving each other; as the Lord has forgiven you, so you also must forgive. And above all these put on love, which binds everything together in perfect harmony. And let the peace of Christ rule in your hearts, to which indeed you were called in one body. And be thankful (Colossians 3:12-15).**

Character: the mental and moral qualities distinctive to an individual. "Running away was not in keeping with her character."

Synonyms: personality, nature, disposition, temperament, temper, mentality, makeup.

The above Webster's Dictionary definition states that character is distinctive to an individual, both mental and moral.

If this definition is true, then how can we all have a Christian character? Wouldn't that make us all the same? God created us in His image, but that does not make us all the same. We are all uniquely gifted, wonderfully made, and special to God, but our character can model that of Christ.

Our character or our personality, temperament, etc. resides in our minds and hearts and is formed from our upbringing. Sometimes, the way we were raised was contrary to the character of Christ, but once we receive Him as our Lord, we become a new creation. The old man is buried with Christ, and a new man rises with Him. Keeping the old man buried required constant attention.

Since our personality or the way we react to the outside world is changed because of Christ, we can have a Christian character by being like-minded with Him and having the same moral code. The old man fights against us, so we must fight to allow Christ's character to become our own.

God became man and dwelt among us so that He could show us how humankind can live in the world and still have a Christian character.

Being found in appearance as a man, He humbled Himself by becoming obedient to the point of death, even death on a cross (Philippians 2:8).

Look at Christ's character. He was humble, He was kind, and He was meek (gentle). He didn't mock people or judge them though He certainly had the right to. I think we can safely say that He was not shy, but He was also not boastful. His nature or His character was loving. His disposition was even and not easily angered. How does that compare to us?

Why do you see the speck that is in your brother's eye, but do not notice the log that is in your own eye? (Matthew 7:3).

The world judges our character. If we are to represent Christ to the lost, we must work hard to think as Christ would. Only with the help of His Holy Spirit can we show the world a better way. We must try, or those around us, even those who ridicule us and judge us for our beliefs, will never come to us for answers or allow us to lead them to salvation. Those who are seeking something positive in their lives will not see it in us. Our Christian character might save a soul.

Christ will take our personalities and mold them into His character in our own unique way, using our personality traits to follow His behavior if we genuinely seek it. This is not easy for any personality type.

When faced with difficult situations, it may seem trite, but we need to ask ourselves what Jesus would say or do. To be like-minded is to have the same thoughts and actions that Christ would have. We have a sinful nature, so we need to stop and think before we act. We must strive to have compassionate hearts and meek (gentle) spirits.

Growing in our relationship with God is the only way to mature and to truly have a Christian character. We do not always want to stay babes in Christ.

Do not be conformed to this world, but be transformed by the renewal of your mind, that by testing you may discern what is the will of God, what is good and acceptable and perfect (Romans 12:2).

Each of Christ's disciples were very different. Some were outgoing, some were trusting, some needed to be shown before believing, and some were arrogant and asked to sit at Christ's right and left hands in glory. God created us as unique individuals because He needed to use these traits to further His work.

God can take our very unique personalities and transform them by renewing our minds. We renew our minds by communicating with Him and reading His word. We must pray in every situation so that we will know what God's will is for us and how we should act and react.

It is vital that we have a Christian character to show this world Christ and His love for us.

> *Prayer:* **Dear Lord, please renew our minds daily so that we will always be focused on you. Help us to behave as Christ would in all situations, never responding in kind with anger or meanness. Let us be loving, gentle and kind to all and do the work that you have called us to do. Amen.**

Fear of Failure

My flesh and my heart may fail, but God is the strength of my heart and my portion forever (Psalm 73:26).

So often we feel that we have failed, not only God, but in life. We've lost jobs, been unsuccessful in our efforts, had marriages or relationships end, and other failures (as the world defines failure).

When we look back at our lives and the relationships that no longer exist or the bad decisions we made, it is difficult to feel good about where we are now. We worry about what others may think of us. We want people to see us as successful. This is *pride.*

Pride is not always a bad thing. We are proud of our accomplishments for God, for finishing something we started, etc. But when pride makes us feel worthless or causes us to pretend that we are something we are not, lying to ourselves and others, then pride becomes a sin, all because we are afraid of being branded a failure.

God has been with us on our journey through the bad decisions, and through the 'failures,' even when we turned away from Him. He has used our decisions for good and to lead us into a closer relationship with Him. If we love the Lord and have chosen Him to lead our lives, then we have succeeded. That is all that God cares about. Knowing Him and making Him known in this world is the only success we need.

Accepting Christ as our Savior is the first major success of our lives. Living our lives by His example is the second. We have succeeded even if we don't feel we are doing much for God. We are going to spend eternity with Him.

Making Him known to others is what the Bible calls *bearing fruit.* Bearing fruit is a great success for God, and sometimes we might not even know when or if it has happened. Living our lives as a light to the world, showing God's love, and doing good for others will bear fruit.

We are not afraid of what the world thinks of us if we are living our lives by Christ's example.

But he said to me, "My grace is sufficient for you, for my power is made perfect in weakness." Therefore I will boast all the more gladly of my weaknesses, so that the power of

> **Christ may rest upon me. For the sake of Christ, then, I am content with weaknesses, insults, hardships, persecutions, and calamities. For when I am weak, then I am strong (2 Corinthians 12:9-10).**

Even if we occasionally fail in our walk with Christ, He never leaves us and never counts us as failures. Jesus spent time in a human body and knows all about our pain and struggles. He was tempted as we are, knows that we are not perfect, and that we will fall. He will help us rise again and keep going.

We can rejoice knowing that, though we think we have failed, God keeps us going with Him as our guide. If we don't lose our salvation, we have succeeded at the greatest task and will spend eternity with Him.

> **Jeremiah, say this to the people of Judah: This is what the Lord says: You know if a man falls down, he gets up again. And if a man goes the wrong way, he turns around and comes back (Jeremiah 8:4).**

If we are going the wrong way, we must turn around and remember what is important. We need to put down our pride in self and turn our eyes to our true life calling. This world will pass away, but what we do for God is eternal. God has forgiven us. We can forgive ourselves and keep going.

> **For the righteous falls seven times and rises again, but the wicked stumble in times of calamity (Proverbs 24:16).**

This sinful world looks down on those they perceive as failures. Family members respect those that succeed and worry about those who have supposedly failed. Wordly failures are sometimes remembered more than successes, but this is all based on the world's view of success and failure.

We see successful people sinning. It has always been this way. Success is often based on money and things instead of gentleness, goodness, and kindness. We may know the difference in our hearts, but we still feel bad about ourselves when we do not meet others' expectations.

Trusting that God has been there all along the road with us, even when we made bad choices, and that He works all things for good for those who love Him, is how we overcome this fear. Instead of hanging our heads in shame, we can thank God for His great gift of saving us and helping us to be of value in a dark and sinful world. We need to rise each time we fall and continue being whom God wants us to be.

When King David was about to die he told Solomon, his son, to follow God and do what God wanted him to do. He didn't tell him to make more money, have a bigger army, or surround himself with gold.

We need to forget about what people think. For the most part, they are so busy thinking about themselves that they may not be thinking about us anyway. Only care what God thinks. Life is not perfect. It is not easy. God promises us heavenly success if we love Him, so that is now our only goal.

***Prayer:* God, show us what true success is in your eyes and help us to strive for that. We rejoice that we have chosen you over the world, but we still fight against our old nature. Let our only care be that we succeed as you view success. Amen.**

Sincerity in Church Worship

But the hour is coming, and is now here, when the true worshipers will worship the Father in spirit and truth, for the Father is seeking such people to worship him (John 4:23).

Many churches do not follow a formal structure and begin service with music and singing. This is generally called the worship service or the song service. It is common these days to have a team of singers and musicians in front of the congregation singing songs and leading the congregation in singing and worship.

This time of singing and worship is a time for us to worship God, who is worthy of our praise. It is a time of rejoicing. It is a time to invite the Holy Spirit to join us in our worship.

It is not the time for preaching or teaching, but a time when our hearts and spirits can commune with the spirit of God. There is nothing harsh or severe. There is no agitation or disagreement, only genial and pleasant songs rising to the Lord…or there should be.

Sing praises to the Lord, for he has done gloriously; let this be made known in all the earth (Isaiah 12:5).

Human beings with difficult lives and different opinions can make these worship times not as smooth as we would like. Age differences in members of the congregation can cause some varied music opinions. Some would prefer a different leader or songs in a different key. The music or the drums are too loud. Why are we clapping? Why aren't we clapping?

Such a special time as a worship service can still be divisive to a church, unless, as worshipers, we make sure that we are sincere in our worship and keep our minds on the One we are worshiping. The music or the key doesn't matter. The drums and other instruments don't matter. Only worshiping God matters and preparing our hearts to hear His word.

God enjoys our worship, no matter how good or how bad it is. Everything we do in worship when we are sincere brings glory and praise to Him.

Make a joyful noise to the Lord, all the earth! Serve the Lord with gladness! Come into his presence with singing! Know that the Lord, he is God! (Psalms 100:1-3).

As members of the congregation, it is our responsibility to stay focused on worshiping the Lord. By joining in the singing, even if we think we are not very good, we encourage those around us to take part. When we sing to the glory of the Lord, not looking around, and not worrying about what others are doing, the Holy Spirit will fall on the congregation, and everyone will feel God's power and presence. Worship service can turn a lost soul to salvation. We don't want to mess it up by having a negative attitude.

Try not to hear every wrong note or every missed chord. If a song is too low or too high, closing our eyes, mouthing the words to ourselves, or praying during worship can gently redirect our mind away from critiquing the singing and the music of others, and back to the words and the worship of the Lord.

Worship leaders must also stay focused on God. Being a worship leader is a heavy responsibility. Their job is to lead the rest of us in spiritual worship with their whole hearts, to help us draw closer to God. They are not performing for us. Our job is not to listen, but to worship.

And David danced before the LORD with all his might, wearing a priestly garment (2 Samuel 6:14).

No matter what style of singing or instruments, no matter how many people are on the platform, there are a few things that we, as the congregation worshiping, need to think about.

First, we need the Holy Spirit to sing through the leaders and through us. We need to see and feel that the team is worshiping and allowing the Holy Spirit's leading. We need to take part. And we need to feel gentle reverence and awe of our great God. Worship time may start fun and fast, but this is not playtime. We are not singing for the sake of singing. We are bringing our offerings of worship before God.

Therefore let us be grateful for receiving a kingdom that cannot be shaken, and thus let us offer to God acceptable worship, with reverence and awe (Hebrews 12:28).

What it all comes down to is us. We need to worship in spirit and in truth. No matter where we are or what is going on around us, it is up to each one of us to worship with sincerity. Others may have different ideas than we do, but it is our responsibility to worship the only one worthy of worship.

And Jesus answered him, "It is written, 'You shall worship the Lord your God, and him only shall you serve'" (Luke 4:8).

***Prayer*: Gentle Father, help us to worship you in spirit and in truth. Remove from us all agitation and frustration over the music. Remove from our minds all concern about our lives. Fill our hearts with love and praise for you. Let your Holy Spirit, who is never harsh but always gentle, fall on the congregation and prepare our hearts to hear your word and to face the world that is before us. Amen.**

Self-Control: The ninth fruit of the Holy Spirit

> **But the fruit of the Spirit is love, joy, peace, patience, kindness, goodness, faithfulness, gentleness, and self-control. Against such things there is no Law. And those who belong to Christ Jesus have crucified the flesh with its passions and desires. If we live by the Spirit, let us also keep in step with the Spirit (Galatians 5:22-25).**

***Egkrateia*: mastery, self-control**

Definition: self-mastery, self-restraint, self-control, continence.

There is not much written about the biblical use of self-control. It is simply dominion from within over something that needs mastering. It proceeds from within, but we cannot do it by ourselves.

'Self-control' – proceeding out from *within* oneself, but *not by oneself.*

For Christians, self-control can only be accomplished by the power of the Holy Spirit. It is mastery over things for which we have no self-control.

> **For this very reason, make every effort to supplement your faith with virtue, and virtue with knowledge, and knowledge with self-control, and self-control with steadfastness, and steadfastness with godliness, and godliness with brotherly affection, and brotherly affection with love (2 Peter 1:5-7).**

> **For God gave us a spirit not of fear but of power and love and self-control (2 Timothy 1:7).**

The God of Self-Control

A man without self-control is like a city broken into and left without walls (Proverbs 25:28).

Without self-control, we have no walls to protect us from thinking or doing things that are not right for us. Unfortunately, we don't think of self-control that often. We just act and react, but God felt it was important enough to give through the Holy Spirit, so we need to sit up and take notice.

All the fruit of the Holy Spirit are given to us for our good to help us grow in God's grace. He wants us to use these fruit in our own lives and also to bring others into the kingdom by showing them to the world. God wants us to produce good fruit, and only a good tree gives forth good fruit. We cannot be a good tree without self-control.

Self-control is last among the fruit, perhaps because we need the other fruit to help us with our self-control. It helps us to be a good tree and to show to others around us that our God is mighty and trustworthy. Scriptures refer to having self-control as it applies to a variety of temptations.

No temptation has overtaken you that is not common to man. God is faithful, and he will not let you be tempted beyond your ability, but with the temptation he will also provide the way of escape, that you may be able to endure it (1 Corinthians 10:13).

Self-control is a tool of the Holy Spirit that uses all the other fruit. It is something we need to exercise so that we are not overtaken by any kind of temptation. This fruit is one of the ways God has provided for escape.

Temptations are different for everyone. Some temptation is sexual or related to addiction. Money and power are temptations. People are self-centered and prideful; seeking fame and recognition. These are all issues Christians combat in everyday life. Without self-control from God, resisting temptations is impossible.

When we know what areas of our lives need self-control, we can ask the Holy Spirit to give this strength in those areas. Since God has provided this way of escape, we can strengthen our Christian walk by relying on God's provision of self-control.

We are running a race day by day, trying to develop a closer, more trusting relationship with our God. We have evil all around, and at every turn something is trying to stop our communion with the Lord. Without His provision of the fruit of self-control, we would surely give in to every temptation.

Trust in God is necessary for self-control. The more we trust Him, the more we strengthen our resolve to serve Him. We believe that overcoming these temptations is what is best for us.

Christ told us that He would send us a helper when He was gone, and that helper is the Holy Spirit. Failing to call on the Holy Spirit when we are struggling is like ignoring a lifeline when drowning.

We are not strong enough in ourselves to have self-control. We are powerless without God in the face of great temptation. We need to run this race wisely with discipline.

> **Do you not know that in a race all the runners run, but only one receives the prize? So run that you may obtain it. Every athlete exercises self-control in all things. They do it to receive a perishable wreath, but we an imperishable. So I do not run aimlessly; I do not box as one beating the air. But I discipline my body and keep it under control, lest after preaching to others I myself should be disqualified (1 Corinthians 9:24-27).**

> ***Prayer:*** **Lord, thank for being the God of self-control. Help us run the race of this world with discipline to win your prize. We know that eternal life is already ours by your sacrifice on the cross, but we want to mature and be the people you want us to be. We ask your Holy Spirit to give us self-control in all things. Help us to acknowledge our weaknesses and to call on your strength with faith to overcome them. Amen.**

Who Are Those Friends Anyway?

Do not be deceived: "Bad company ruins good morals" (1 Corinthians 15:33).

How many friends do we have that we can call true? How many are Christians and live a lifestyle that is pleasing to God? Can we tell them anything and call on them at any time?

Although our non-Christian friends may be true, we tend to behave differently around them, especially if they have strong feelings about religion. With our Christian friends, we do not have to tread lightly about our beliefs.

If being around non-Christian friends causes us to change our language and behavior, something is not right, either in the friendship itself, or in our relationship with God.

Today's friendships, and I use the term loosely, are very different from friendships of the past. When social media came on the scene, we began to reveal more details about ourselves than ever before.

So-called 'Facebook friends,' some of whom we have never met, post their political beliefs (that we didn't ask them about), pictures of their hospital visits, injuries, meals, (all of which we may not care to see), opinions about other people, fights, likes, and dislikes. They share things from others who are not our 'friends' that is full of vile language and pictures, and they say things that, hopefully, they would never say in person.

How many 'friends' do we have on Facebook? Do we think about who they really are and what they believe? Do we even know them? How much self-control are we exercising while on social media?

Do we think seriously about what we post? Even employers check Facebook these days to see what kind of people we are. Christians need to consider these things and how they affect our faith and our witness. Social media is one place where self-control is crucial.

A man of many companions may come to ruin, but there is a friend who sticks closer than a brother (Proverbs 18:24).

Jesus is the friend who sticks closer than a brother. He is always true. We can take our every care to Him. He is always 'online' and will never block us or unfriend us. Communicating constantly with Him is a lifeline for us in this world but also requires self-control over the other things that take our time away from Him.

Not only do we need to have self-control over what we post on social media, but also over the amount of time we spend there. Have we really been waiting all these years to have a place to spill our most personal thoughts and actions in public? Do we really feel better when we do?

The better way would be to control what we put on social media, and instead of posting for the world, take everything to Christ and to our Christian friends, who will bear our burdens with us.

Bear one another's burdens, and so fulfill the law of Christ (Galatians 6:2).

Bearing one another's burdens is best done in the privacy of each other's company, not online, where the world can see our posts and where they stay for a very long time. Attending church is a great place to make friends that are true. Christ encourages us to connect in person, but we often hide behind the social media veil.

The world is changing, and trying to keep up by using technology may not always be the best course of action. We lack self-control when we spend many hours looking at posts from people we don't know when we could be interacting with God or a Christian friend. If we must use technology, we can use it to read God's word.

And let us consider how to stir up one another to love and good works, not neglecting to meet together, as is the habit of some, but encouraging one another, and all the more as you see the Day drawing near (Hebrews 10:24-25).

Social media is not going away anytime soon, but we can encourage each other to exercise self-control in its use. If we find it difficult to cut down on our visits to social media sites or our use of cell phones, we need to ask for self-control from our heavenly Father. God's voice does not want to be drowned out by the masses.

For what does it profit a man if he gains the whole world and loses or forfeits himself? (Luke 9:25).

Time spent with friends that share our beliefs and lifestyle will lift us up. We do not want to be divided between the world and Christ. Friends are great, but Christian friends are brothers and sisters in the body of Christ.

When worldly temptations come along, we must seek wisdom from the Holy Spirit. Self-control over our social media habit can only come from God and an awareness of the pitfalls of overuse.

***Prayer*: Lord, the world is moving fast. Keeping up with technology can take our minds off you and your plan for our lives. Give us self-control and wisdom to know how to use all the tools that the world is providing us. Help us to use them to further your kingdom. Amen.**

Christian Triggers

> **Watch and pray that you may not enter into temptation. The spirit indeed is willing, but the flesh is weak (Matthew 26:41).**

We call them triggers. Triggers are places, people, things, smells, events, etc. that cause us to want to do something we know is wrong. Our flesh is weak.

For example, the smell of alcohol to an alcoholic may trigger a desire to drink. Those in recovery are taught to stay away from bars and places where this trigger might be. Being around smokers would be difficult for people who have quit smoking. Chocolate cake may be a trigger for someone on a diet.

As Christians, we want to stay away from all sin, but some give us difficulty. We may even justify to ourselves that these activities aren't really sin (and some are not), but God's word is clear about doing wrong.

We should acknowledge our triggers and try to stay away from them if we truly want success at overcoming our weaknesses and being a better person. Self-control given to us by the Holy Spirit will give us strength from within to overcome these triggers.

> **Now the works of the flesh are evident: sexual immorality, impurity, sensuality, idolatry, sorcery, enmity, strife, jealousy, fits of anger, rivalries, dissensions, divisions, envy, drunkenness, orgies, and things like these. I warn you, as I warned you before, that those who do such things will not inherit the kingdom of God (Galatians 5:19-21).**

What we call triggers, the Bible calls temptation. We often find ourselves in situations that tempt us to sin. A movie may have sexually explicit material we weren't expecting. We may continually shop online when we know we have an obsession with (worship) clothes, cars, purses, etc.

Some have their palms read 'just for fun' or attend parties where there will be a lot of drinking and drugs. Co-workers 'innocently flirt' at work, online, or in texting when they are married. Sin surrounds us. Only by employing self-control from God, with our own wish to stand strong, will we be able to withstand the tricks of the devil.

> **But each person is tempted when he is lured and enticed by his own desire (James 1:14).**

After identifying our weaknesses and the triggers or temptations that draw us to them, we ask God to deliver us from what is luring us away from Him to our own desires.

> **And he said, "What comes out of a person is what defiles him. For from within, out of the heart of man, come evil thoughts, sexual immorality, theft, murder, adultery, coveting, wickedness, deceit, sensuality, envy, slander, pride, foolishness. All these evil things come from within, and they defile a person" (Mark 7:20-23).**

The works of the flesh are sin, and what comes from our evil thoughts is sin, and yet we set ourselves up by being around temptations. Although some situations are beyond our control, we should remove ourselves as soon as possible.

The world may think it is progressing, but God is the same yesterday, today and forever. Sin is sin. People surround us who don't think any of these things are wrong, but we know the truth. Christians should not be like those who seek only their own pleasure and self-satisfaction. We seek to please God and to live according to His word. We must be truthful with God and with ourselves about the things of this world that tempt us.

> **Whoever conceals his transgressions will not prosper, but he who confesses and forsakes them will obtain mercy (Proverbs 28:13).**

We need to surround ourselves with like-minded people. We can't get out of living in the world until the Lord takes us home, but we don't have to participate in sinful behavior. We must exercise self-control with prayer.

> **If we say we have no sin, we deceive ourselves, and the truth is not in us. If we confess our sins, he is faithful and**

just to forgive us our sins and to cleanse us from all unrighteousness. If we say we have not sinned, we make him a liar, and his word is not in you (1 John 1: 8-10).

Prayer: **God, please forgive us when we fall into temptation. We will confess our sins and sincerely try to give them up. We ask you to help us as we struggle in this evil world. Your Holy Spirit is with us. Thank you for your fruit of self-control. Amen.**

Christians Make Mistakes

For we all stumble in many ways. And if anyone does not stumble in what he says, he is a perfect man, able also to bridle his whole body (James 3:2).

Christians make mistakes. We are far from perfect. Every day we do, say, or think something that we know is not Godly. We are frustrated at the car in front of us on the road. We are judgmental about someone we come across or something we hear. We might join in with office gossip or whine about our boss. We might be angry at our husbands or wives or think of a way to lie and not get caught.

We stumble, but we don't fall because God holds us up. He gives us self-control when it would be easy to make a mistake. However, if we don't listen to Him or stop and think before we act, we will continue to make mistakes and may cause hurt and anger.

Self-control must be exercised and is not our natural state, but the more we talk to God about it and live our lives as representatives of Him, the more self-control we will have.

Surely there is not a righteous man on earth who does good and never sins (Ecclesiastes 7:20).

If we accept that we make mistakes but don't learn from them or try to avoid them, we will not grow closer to God. Not moving closer to God is actually moving farther away. We need to let our conscience guide us and ask God to help us overcome these constant mistakes by making us aware of them.

But the Helper, the Holy Spirit, whom the Father will send in my name, he will teach you all things and bring to your remembrance all that I have said to you (John 14:26).

If we want to be more like Christ, we cannot do it alone. We need the Holy Spirit to speak to us each time we are about to make one of these mistakes so that we can control our thoughts and actions.

We often forget to rely on or call on the Holy Spirit for self-control when we are struggling with mistakes, temptation, and sin. Remember that Jesus not only died on the cross so that we would be forgiven and have eternal life with Him, He also did not leave us alone to fend for ourselves. He gave us His Holy Spirit.

> **Whoever conceals his transgressions will not prosper, but he who confesses and forsakes them will obtain mercy (Proverbs 28:13).**

It is not news to us that we make mistakes, and it shouldn't surprise us when God brings them to our awareness. That is what conscience is for. We are not hiding anything from God, and yet He wants us to bring our transgressions to Him and ask for his forgiveness.

Many of our mistakes reflect on Christianity and may affect our personal lives at work or with our families.

God wants us to succeed, not as the world views success, but as He views success. When we confess our mistakes to Him and learn to control our impulses, He has mercy on us, and we will prosper in our Christian walk.

God knows the world. He knows the struggles we face every day. There is nothing new under the sun, and the mistakes we make will never surprise God. He is with us and will strengthen our self-control with His righteous right hand.

> **Fear not, for I am with you; be not dismayed, for I am your God; I will strengthen you, I will help you, I will uphold you with my righteous right hand (Isaiah 41:10).**

> ***Prayer*: Lord, help us in all situations to do as Christ would do and not what comes to our natural minds. Strengthen our self-control so that we make fewer mistakes, especially those that reflect badly on you. We trust that you will not allow harm to come to anyone because of our mistakes. Teach and guide us, Lord. Amen.**

Wandering Minds

You keep him in perfect peace whose mind is stayed on you, because he trusts in you (Isaiah 26:3).

When we pray, sometimes our minds wander to other parts of our lives. We start to think about what we did during the day or what is going to happen in the future. Then we snap back to our prayer and feel bad because we weren't focused on God and what we were praying about.

It is difficult to exercise self-control when we pray. God understands that this world is sometimes overwhelming in what it requires of us. He knows our minds are continually moving.

Wherever our minds wander during prayer and communication with God, that can become part of our prayer. It makes us aware of what is burdening us, and though God already knows about it, He enjoys it when we bring those things to Him.

When our minds return to prayer, we should talk to God about our wandering off and let Him know what is weighing on our minds. Self-control is not just about resisting temptation. It is also available for us when we need to stay focused on Christ.

If our minds wander to sinful thoughts, we need to take those thoughts captive and ask for forgiveness and more self-control. We walk in the flesh, but we can walk with the Spirit.

We are living in a sinful world. We are not waging war against other people, though it may seem so at times. We are fighting the powers of darkness who are out to destroy us. One of the ways we are destroyed is by allowing our thoughts to remain on things of this world and not of Christ.

Praise God, we have the Holy Spirit to guide and instruct us as we fight this battle. The fruit of self-control, though not the most talked about, is one of the most important fruits we can ask for. In our own power, we cannot fight what causes our minds to wander, but with self-control, we can keep our mind focused on the Lord.

For though we walk in the flesh, we are not waging war according to the flesh. For the weapons of our warfare are not of the flesh but have divine power to destroy strongholds. We

destroy arguments and every lofty opinion raised against the knowledge of God, and take every thought captive to obey Christ, being ready to punish every disobedience, when your obedience is complete (2 Corinthians 10:3-6).

When our minds wander in prayer to our grocery list, that is one thing, but when it wanders to hate and anger toward a co-worker, that is when we need self-control. Those are the issues to bring before the Lord, asking for forgiveness and for the ability to love and show His love.

If we are waiting to spend time in prayer until we are tired and stressed out from our day, our minds are more likely to wander.

If our minds wander when someone is talking to us, they will surely realize that we are not paying attention. Communication is how we have relationships that are sustainable.

Communication with God is the same. God will never give up on being our friend, no matter how often our minds wander, but we cannot have a sustainable, close relationship with Him if our minds wander off when we are in the middle of a conversation.

He is a double-minded man, unstable in all his ways (James 1:8).

A person whose mind is always wandering off or thinking about their own issues and activities is not focused on God. We can easily become double-minded and unstable Christians. Our goal as Christians should always be to continually mature and draw closer in our relationship with God.

Prayer: **Lord, help us be aware when our minds are beginning to wander. Help us reign in our thoughts and discuss our worries with you. We ask your Holy Spirit for self-control and to help us practice self-control when we are talking to you. Lead us into greater and deeper prayer to strengthen our relationship with you. Amen.**

Out of Our Control

"Look," said Naomi, "your sister-in-law is going back to her people and her gods. Go back with her." But Ruth replied, "Don't urge me to leave you or to turn back from you. Where you go I will go, and where you stay I will stay. Your people will be my people and your God my God. Where you die I will die, and there I will be buried. May the LORD deal with me, be it ever so severely, if even death separates you and me." When Naomi realized that Ruth was determined to go with her, she stopped urging her. So the two women went on until they came to Bethlehem (Ruth 1:15-19).

There is a great lesson in the story of Ruth and Naomi in the Bible that we should try to put into practice. The lesson is that we should not complain about what we can't control, so we should control what we can and leave the rest to God.

There is so much in life that is out of our control, yet we try to hold control tightly. When we can't control something, or we don't know what is going to happen in a situation, we become frustrated and fearful. Where is our trust in God?

The story says Ruth and Naomi's husbands had died, so the women went to Bethlehem during the famine. They were poor and alone. There is so much more to the story, but we want to concentrate on Ruth.

Ruth did not complain about her situation. She did not consider herself a victim, and she did not pine over what the future might hold. There were no 'what ifs' in Ruth's life.

There was very little that Ruth, a Moabite, could do to survive in Bethlehem, but she took control of what she could. She gleaned in the fields of barley and wheat to feed herself and her mother-in-law, and she left the rest up to God.

Little did Ruth know that God was working behind the scenes to set her up with a fantastic future that would change the course of history. God is working behind the scenes of our lives, too.

It is important for us to realize that, like Ruth, if we take control of what we can control and leave the rest to God, He will continue working on our behalf to give what is best for us and we do not need to worry or fret. Self-control helps us to stop trying to control what we can't and shouldn't control.

Trying to control what is out of our control is painful, takes up too much of our thoughts and emotions, and isn't successful. If we tell ourselves daily to control what we can and leave the rest to God, we will have greater peace and will learn to trust Him more as we see Him move in our lives.

When we look back at our pasts at the last thing we tried to control that didn't work out, we realize our ability to control is very limited. Learning to trust that God is in control is better. It may sound strange, but it takes a lot of self-control to give up control and trust God. Choosing to say, "Your will be done" is difficult, but the more we say it, the more we will mean it.

> **"For I know the plans I have for you," declares the Lord, "plans to prosper you and not to harm you, plans to give you hope and a future" (Jeremiah 29:11).**

It is spiritually valuable to us to try to be like Ruth and step out of our situation, only taking control of the things we can control, and exercising our self-control by leaving the rest to God. He is working on our behalf. We can trust in Him.

> ***Prayer:*** **Lord, help me take my hands off my life when you are working for my good. Help me to take the steps that you want me to take, to control what you want me to control, and to give me self-control so that I can leave the rest to you. Amen.**

The Bible is Important

All Scripture is God-breathed and is useful for teaching, rebuking, correcting and training in righteousness (2 Timothy 3:16).

We read the Bible, we quote the Bible, and we say we believe in the Bible. Why is the Bible so important? Why should we read it every day and believe what its pages say? Why are we instructed to share the word of God?

Christians believe that these writings were inspired by God. Therefore, we say it is the word of God and, for us, that is the reason we should read it. Most importantly to the Christian, the writings from the Old Testament foretold the coming of Christ, His birth, and where, when and how He would die. The Old Testament lays out God's plan to bring man back into a close relationship with Him.

The New Testament shows that all those prophecies came true and goes on to teach and explain the life God wants us to live. God's words are the most important words we will ever read.

God's word is how we know about His plan. It is how we know about the dangers that face us because of Satan's fall from grace. It is how we know about the Old Testament sacrifices that led to Jesus as the 'once for all' final sacrifice on the cross for our sins. It is how we understand that through His death and resurrection, we can stand before God as new creations.

From the beginning of the Old Testament to the Crucifixion and resurrection of Jesus in our place, we can see how God brought us back from the fall of Adam and Eve, taught us about His love for us, and ultimately gives us eternal life with Him if we believe and accept this gift and ask Him to forgive our sins.

You must understand that no prophecy of Scripture came about by the prophet's own interpretation. For prophecy never had its origin in the will of man, but men spoke from God as they were carried along by the Holy Spirit (2 Peter 1:20,21).

Reading the word is wonderful, but God has told us to also share it because of its great worth. God used the Holy Spirit through people like us to write His story, and now He uses us to teach His story to those who don't know the truth.

We often avoid telling our friends and relatives about God's word. Even though it is our responsibility to shine the light of God's love to a lost and dying world, it takes great self-control not to run from opportunities to share the good news. Fear of sharing the gospel is common even among the most mature.

Controlling our fear and developing the ability to talk to people about why His word is important is given to us by God. He will tell us when to speak, how to speak, and will give us the boldness to speak.

First, though, we must know the story, have a grasp of God's plan, and know why the word of God is important. To know God and to show God should be our motto and we can only show God if we know Him. We know Him by reading His word and communicating through prayer.

> **Everything that was written in the past was written to teach us, so that through endurance and the encouragement of the Scriptures we might have hope (Romans 15:4).**

We have hope through the encouraging words in the Bible and the teachings that they hold. Those who don't believe in Christ may never have heard or understood His word. They are looking for hope in this world, and we can give it to them.

God's word gives us hope while we struggle with the problems of this world. We can't keep this to ourselves. We can share our own personal struggles and how God has worked in our lives. We can develop the self-control that it will take for us to step out of our comfort zone and speak up. We do not have to be Bible scholars.

Some will say to us that "the Bible is contradictory in places." To respond to statements like this, we need to know the writer of the Bible passage, to whom they are writing, and when and why it was being written. If we understand these, we will find that there are no contradictions in the Bible.

Some might say, "The Bible is not literal." Others will say, "The Bible is absolutely literal." The truth is that the Bible is both literal in places and figurative in places. As Jesus used parables to teach, so the Bible uses literal and figurative words to help us understand. We should use knowledge and common sense when reading God's word and when sharing.

If we feel that there is a contradiction, we do not understand God's word and should seek clarity from someone who knows more. It is acceptable to say to a nonbeliever, "That is a good question, I will find out the answer and get back to you."

God, Jesus, the Holy Spirit, and God's word will never contradict each other, but if we don't understand it clearly, we could find ourselves in uncomfortable conversations. We are not taught the scriptures as people were long ago when the Bible was the basis for all education. It is unfortunate. We must hear the word at church and study on our own, which takes a great deal of self-control.

> **You know how, when you were a small child, you were taught the holy Scriptures; and it is these that make you wise to accept God's salvation by trusting in Christ Jesus (2 Timothy 3:15).**

In 2 Timothy 3, Paul reminds Timothy that he was not to take anything away from or add anything to the scriptures that he had learned from his mother as a child, nor from anything Paul had taught him.

This scripture applies to us also. Reading the scriptures (the Bible) make us wise and knowledgeable about the salvation that comes from Christ, and knowledge is power when sharing God's word.

> *Prayer:* **Father, give us insight and understanding when we read your word, so that we can explain it to others. Give us boldness to speak and self-control not to let those opportunities pass us by. Speak through us so that others will know your love and follow you. Amen.**

Our Sinful Nature

For all have sinned and fall short of the glory of God (Romans 3:23).

According to Strong's Concordance the original New Testament Greek for sin is ***ἁμαρτία*** *(hamartia) and means failure, being in error, missing the mark; offense, wrong-doing, misdeed.*

When we think of sin, we concentrate mostly on the last two definitions listed above, i.e., wrong-doing and misdeed, but the others are important, too. Failure in following Christ's teaching, being in error in how we behave or what we say, and missing the mark in our beliefs about what is sin, can and do have serious consequences. The Bible is very clear when talking about sin.

For I know that nothing good dwells in me, that is, in my flesh. For I have the desire to do what is right, but not the ability to carry it out (Romans 7:18).

We are born with a sinful nature, i.e., 'the flesh.' We want, like Paul, to do what is right but our flesh fights against our spirit. Thanks to God, we have the Holy Spirit to help us.

Though we are a selfish and perverse people who want what we want when we want it, we know what is right in God's sight. Self-control of any kind is not considered necessary in today's sinful world, but we want self-control because Christians are not of this world and we want to please God, who created us.

But understand this, that in the last days there will come times of difficulty. For people will be lovers of self, lovers of money, proud, arrogant, abusive, disobedient to their parents, ungrateful, unholy, heartless, unappeasable, slanderous, without self-control, brutal, not loving good, treacherous, reckless, swollen with conceit, lovers of pleasure rather than lovers of God, having the appearance of godliness, but denying its power. Avoid such people (2 Timothy 3:1-5).

This describes the world today. 'It's all about me' is the way of life today. We have so much freedom to choose what we do and where we go, that we concentrate all our efforts on ourselves. That feeds our sinful nature.

We are not perfect, but we recognize and acknowledge our sin and ask God for forgiveness. We must decide not to repeat our wrong-doings and fight against our sinful nature. This is when we must ask God for self-control.

> **Jesus answered them, "Truly, truly, I say to you, everyone who commits sin is a slave to sin" (John 8:34).**

If we are continually sinning, we may need to seek professional help. This can come in many forms such as first admitting we have a problem, seeking counsel, medication, prayer, changing our lifestyles, and/or giving up some of the people we hang out with.

> **So, whoever knows that right thing to do and fails to do it, for him it is sin (James 4:17).**

Whatever our struggles are, if we know the right thing to do, and we fail to do it, for us it is sin. With the help of God, the Holy Spirit and our Christian brothers and sisters, we can fully experience Christ's abundant life. The joy of the Lord is better than being a slave to sin.

> **If we say we have no sin, we deceive ourselves, and the truth is not in us. If we confess our sins, he is faithful and just to forgive us our sins and to cleanse us from all unrighteousness. If we say we have not sinned, we make him a liar, and his word is not in us (1 John 1:8-10).**

We must be brutally honest with ourselves about our sinful nature. The world offers many opportunities that seem fun and enticing. Many of our friends, even Christian friends, partake of these activities. However, we can only judge what is right and wrong for us.

The news or social media tries to convince us that certain behaviors are acceptable. The Bible tells us what sin is and what it is not, and our spirit and our conscience will confirm.

Or do you not know that the unrighteous will not inherit the kingdom of God? Do not be deceived: neither the sexually immoral, nor idolaters, nor adulterers, nor men who practice homosexuality, nor thieves, nor the greedy, nor drunkards, nor revilers, nor swindlers will inherit the kingdom of God (1 Corinthians 6:9-10).

***Prayer*: Lord, help us separate ourselves from the world and keep our eyes on you. Strengthen our self-control when we are tempted and surrounded by sin that is considered acceptable in today's world. On our own, we cannot be strong enough, but with your Holy Spirit, we can overcome. Amen.**

Made in the USA
San Bernardino, CA
06 December 2018